Stand in My Window

STAND IN

MY WINDOW

Meditations on Home and How We Make It

LaTonya Yvette

THE DIAL PRESS • NEW YORK

Published in the United States by the Dial Press, an imprint of Random House, a division of Penguin Random House LLC, New York.

THE DIAL PRESS is a registered trademark and the colophon is a trademark of Penguin Random House LLC.

ISBN: 9780593242414
EBOOK ISBN: 9780593242421

Printed in China on acid-free paper

randomhousebooks.com

9 8 7 6 5 4 3 2 1

First Edition

Book design by Arsh Raziuddin

The word *ecology* is derived from the Greek *oikos,*
the word for home.

—Robin Wall Kimmerer, *Braiding Sweetgrass*

For Mom,
Grandma,
Great-Grandma,
my sister,
my daughter,
and all the
women who have
taught me how
to return home

Contents

Introd

uction

When people pass away, I say to my children, *May their memory be a blessing.* I do this as a way to codify who they were, and the eternal message we will graciously be gifted just by holding on to their memory. I recited these same words as we were forced to say goodbye to our apartment of five years in Brooklyn, a place that felt like a bridge of healing from who I was to who I wanted to be. This home on Clinton Avenue cradled me as I split from my ex-husband. It held my four-year-old son through the healing process of open-heart surgery. It helped define my life as a writer, sheltered our family through the very worst of the pandemic in New York City, and comforted me through another breakup and subsequent depression. *May its memory be a blessing.*

But this grief over our lost home coincided with the blessing of a new one. As we closed the doors behind us on Clinton Avenue, we opened the rust-red doors to the Mae House, a nearly two-hundred-year-old home at the bed of the Hudson, in a tiny village in the Catskills, a place I purchased as the pandemic subsided to not only call my own but to teach and liberate me. This house is our future, but like all living things, it bears a history—a memory—of its own. It's the same way that even my future is upheld by those gone before me: my family, yes, but also those women from the past who made an indelible mark on who I am—from Audre Lorde and Angela Davis to the nineteenth-century washerwomen who were the first to fight for fair wages for their labor, and so many more. My future is made by all the Black, Indigenous people of color who have carefully, thoughtfully made their homes—driven in their souls by their own aspirations and ambitions; their memories of the past and reflections toward the future.

Over the last three years, the idea of this book has transformed. It began as an exploration of Christine Blasey Ford's accusation against then Supreme Court nominee Brett Kavanaugh. It stuck with me that, due to sexual assault,

her orientation to home lacked safety. While she made national news, my first book, *Woman of Color*, had just been released, and I knew I had edited pieces of my story to fit neatly between the book's pages. Ford's case led me to Anita Hill's testimony against Supreme Court judge Clarence Thomas in 1991, which took place when I was only two. I watched the videos of her testimony and they felt so familiar. It wasn't just Ford, not just Hill; it was the repeating story of a young woman having to prove something had been done to disrupt her sense of safety, of self—of home. Ford combed through her story with excruciating detail; Hill distinctly did not. However different the measures each of these women took, and whatever way women in general build safe homes for ourselves in response to, or in spite of, dangerous transgressions, Angela Davis's words ring true: "Freedom is a constant struggle!"

I once was told by my ex-partner after years of sharing stories and thoughts that I had at least five books in me. I am still unsure of the quantity or the quality of that statement, but I think here, too, of Toni Morrison's famous 1981 speech to the Ohio Arts Council: "If there's a book that you want to read, but it hasn't been written yet, then you must write it." And so, my work evolved into what you now hold in your hands—a book that explores the connection between home and safety, and the migration between the two. It is a reflection of what we inherit, what we pass to our children, and the safe spaces we can create with our hands, within our bodies, and of course, deep in our souls.

In the process of writing this book and bringing the Mae House to fruition, I also turned to the words of prison abolitionist Mariame Kaba:

> One of the things I always talk about is the importance of your individual traumas being transformed into political commitments.
>
> Here's an example of what I mean. So I'm a survivor of rape. And I was a reactionary survivor. . . . I wanted revenge. That was

important. I had to process that . . . [But you] have to think about the political commitment you develop from the experience you've had that's a personal and harmful experience and then you have to think about how to apply that across the board to multiple people and major different contexts.

Kaba's words resonated with me, if only as a reminder that my experience can stretch beyond its isolation of and in my body. What I've learned over time, not in just speaking with people but in living, is that so much of what I write here holds collective resonance. I can choose not to research and write what you're about to read (which would be easier in some regard). Or I can do it and in the process not only dare to liberate myself a bit but have that liberation be part of a political practice and commitment that may affect people.

Writing this book has not been easy. It has disrupted my sleep and my family's routines. It has made me deeply uncomfortable. It has upended the way I see our bodies, our homes, and the objects we keep within them. I put pen to paper with heavy thoughts swirling: the pandemic, climate change, the migration of refugees, the impediment of our rights as women. I started to write right as I began sowing my own roots, reaching for my own American Dream with the Mae House: becoming a homeowner in my early thirties. Where I hoped to find comfort in this new time, I found questions. Where I hoped to feel steady and settled, I found an active liberation. This confluence of events reminded me of those fulcrum moments in my own past, transitioning from childhood to adulthood and finding my mother, my grandmother, doing the same. Writing helped me maintain the hope that exists outside of these big historical events, simply because we are tasked with generating hope always.

It also created in me a voracious appetite for information on home from different axes and sources.

For generations, we as people—I refer here mostly to Black people—have reimagined and built upon our history and hope for the future to create *home*. This has not been an easy task, for the many difficult and disparate reasons that this book explores. I have had to meditate my way through the writing process, constantly considering its purpose.

In meditation, there is a connection between body and space: the floor, my room, the weighted pillow I hold, or even the sounds of the city or the quiet land of the Mae House. There is breath, thought, the waviness of both. Through meditation, I have learned to allow things to be as they are, without judgment or a search for resolution. And miraculously, there is a sense of peace.

That is why *Stand in My Window* is not just a collection of essays centered on the topic of home. It is a collection of meditations about home. After years of its faithful companionship, I pass this book on to you. I worry about its place in this changing world, about what it will mean, years from now, when I am changed again. When this fear creeps in, I pause, sit cross-legged on my floor, palms up, open to receive, and listen to the gathering of hums that told me then while writing, and that tells me now while sending it to you, "Welcome home."

If i stand in my window

naked in my own house

and press my breasts

against the windowpane

like black birds pushing against glass

because i am somebody

in a New Thing

and if the man come to stop me

in my own house

naked in my own window

saying i have offended him

i have offended his

Gods

let him watch my black body

push against my own glass

let him discover self

let him run naked through the streets

crying

praying in tongues

—Lucille Clifton

Desahogar

VENT \ TO UN—DROWN \ HOME

When I was seven years old, my parents took us to view an apartment, just two or three out of us five kids, in the suburbs of Long Island. I don't remember much about the place, but I do remember the rooms felt like cubicles, perfectly square windows with tiny sills, cupped and scuffed hardwood floors throughout. As we left and got out of earshot from the real estate agent, my mom said, "Daddy could do the floors!" It was all I needed to hear to believe that we could make the new place work for us if the landlords allowed.

My parents scurried ahead and started discussing logistics. Where I saw resistance in my father's body, I saw excitement in my mother's. Later, I got a whiff of a possible disagreement—bad credit, an issue with a family member—something that didn't make sense at the time but in hindsight created an obtuse line between us being a family that could live in that house and one that couldn't. At that point, it had been a few weeks of hopping around, my parents rotating children to see each new space (because no potential landlord wants to imagine five children in a house)—and we needed something, anything, relatively close to a place to call home.

I'm not sure why my mother's words from that sunny afternoon stuck with me. Especially considering that for most of my life, home has been any place where my three brothers, my sister, my mother, and I resided together. I suspect the power was in the way she sounded so sure of herself. My parents' credit issues, their many children, and even the house's lack of rooms were not detriments to her. She saw something we could work with. Whatever seemed to be less than ideal, *we* would make beautiful.

Over the years, I learned that my father, a Panamanian man who migrated to New York City when he was a tween, was known for his ability to make an old floor look new. He had a buffing machine that stood half as tall as his frame and sounded like a car motor. A day of waxing, another day of sealing with a polyurethane wood finish, and the floor would look brand-new. Floors were one of his specialties. When my dad was estranged from us and we continued to move around, my mother would attack problematic floors herself, finding her own solutions. Her method was easier: a really good scrub with a mop—or better, on her hands and knees—a light screening, and a new coat of wax. We'd watch as she would transform the floors over the course of a day, leaning her pear-shape body into the pin-thin mop, stepping back to appreciate her work again and again. The coat would last for a year, and then she would return to the floor and do it all over again, perfecting her work with each pass. In every home, she did this, on her own. She never complained. Instead, her message was consistent: things would be taken care of if we took care of them.

My mother was in her thirties then, the same age I am now raising my two children, so my memories have the clarity of comparison. She must have felt then the same way I do now, because my grandmother was present with her, taking on the beauty of home with the same fortitude. My grandmother Bertha's apartment was unchanged for seventeen years, save for the addition of an empty adjacent apartment once her neighbor passed away. My uncle, my aunt, and my baby cousin called the other apartment home. My family stayed there, too, when we visited Brooklyn.

And whenever a storm rolled in over Brooklyn during those visits, we were told to go to an enclosed room, turn off the lights, and sit in stillness while my grandmother prayed aloud about God's timing and order. Despite her assertion that we should be, she was hardly ever still—even going so far as to lay red bricks on the wall of her living room with my uncle over the course of a few days. When the beautiful brick wall was done, she returned her attention to the objects in her kitchen that were meticulously arranged and dusted them with a thin piece of Bounty she had previously used, dried, and would reuse again if it did not tear.

My grandmother, like my mother, often made casual remarks about money,

New York City, and living below one's means, but to me, the way she lived was extravagant and abundant. The thrift store was an expensive department store, and that random chair from the garbage was a piece befitting a museum. "A shame someone threw this out!" These treasures were possessed of their own mysterious stories—just like my grandmother was, in my view, and even my mother. On paper, my grandmother loved Jesus, she was an impeccable teacher, a writer, and a deeply regarded member of her Prospect Heights community. Who she was off paper appeared in fleeting but massive moments of one-on-one time, in which a passive sentence became a narrative. Her possessions added to the secret story of who she was. She died when I was eighteen, and my family picked up this legacy.

The following year, my father passed away. I lost a grandparent and a parent in quick succession, and I watched my mother shrink as if two parts of herself had been carried off with them. My daughter was born soon after their deaths, and I entered motherhood myself while my own mother was reduced by her grief. I realize now that my mother and I were made the same, resolving our memory of the past while parenting into the future.

In those early years of motherhood, I pretended my father was just somewhere else, like Florida, changing the oil under the hood of his blue hooptie, his laugh rattling through the motor. And my grandmother I preserved in pieces, her possessions inhabiting my own tiny two-bedroom railroad apartment: a record player, a side table, an assortment of her ornaments. My mother visited my home back then, but where there should have been an intimacy in my newfound womanhood as a mother, there was a unique distance. Our relationship had changed. I tried to hang on to my childhood memory of her through her advice, taking care of something and calling it my own.

Throughout my childhood, my mother's practice of making things nice maddened me, especially if we were in the middle of an eviction process. I witnessed what I felt to be her delusion carrying on right up until a scheduled court date or the night before an eviction. Then, with sudden urgency, she gathered us together to hurriedly pack or collect money for our temporary stay or new home. Still, there were group cleans and large meals on a Sunday when we made it. At other moments between, it was flipping through catalogs, where we could point to furniture we could customize, or planning layouts at Rent-A-Center, blasting the familiarity of Faith Evans from the front seat of the car with the windows down, or making sure our hair and outfits were never out of place.

Now I see that she did not allow us to be reduced to chaos; rather, she enabled us with a peculiar kind of magic. A magic that enabled my vision and fostered my need to inspect homemaking, homegoing, and this body—our bodies—with curiosity.

Fire Season

Suppression of our natural responses to disaster is part of the disease of our time. The refusal to acknowledge these responses causes a dangerous splitting. It divorces our mental calculations from our intuitive, emotional, and biological embeddedness in the matrix of life. That split allows us passively to acquiesce in the preparations for our own demise.

—ROBIN WALL KIMMERER

The stick of palo santo I light every morning stands rigid with slightly charred ends, a memory within a memory of being set to fire several times over the week. The ends darken gray over time, and, once lit with a *whoosh* and three starter clicks of the stove, the stick seems to recall what to do once again. I let the fire travel across it; watching as it catches shreds of splintering wood, then crackles, releasing two or three embers that float, then dissolve on my broken white tile kitchen floor. Soon after lighting, the flame transitions from red to black, then extinguishes itself, but not without leaving a trail of smoke that smells of earth and lemon at once. I place the palo santo stick on my window ledge no matter the season and remove anything that inhibits the smoke's ability to travel the room. The fire is out, but the smoke acts like a body charting its own path, finding corners to settle into and call home.

Native people believe that palo santo aids with bodily elements like depression, anxiety, and inflammation, and its antioxidant-rich phytochemicals, called *terpenes*, are said to be the "lifeblood." Palo santo is known also as *holy wood*, and its composition only doubles its popularity of use. For me and my home, I use it to cleanse the energy from the outside spirits that occasionally make their way in, while also, hopefully, relieving my often achy body from its usual morning joint calls. If my son, Oak, catches me in the process of lighting it, he quickly asks me to explain the difference between blue fire and red fire; which one hurts more, lights faster, burns more furiously. I calm his questions with the truth that I know easily: fire does what it needs to. Handled with care, we can watch it with reverence without knowing the intricate details of its labor. Knowing doesn't distill its work in our home and the homes of others. It exists and moves freely as a form of care, destruction, and ultimately, celebration, whether we consent to it or not.

Technically, there are several elements to Oak's query, factors such as temperature, fuel composition, and oxygen proportion during the combustion. The blue fire of my gas burner is said to reach upward of two thousand degrees, a complete combustion. But when the fire is transferred from the stove to the stick, it is visibly red, lowering to nearly one thousand degrees Fahrenheit, single-handedly transforming the properties of the flame. I observe how the fire on the stick shortens it with every use, and it smells a little less powerful with each burn. Whenever my palo santo gets down to a nub, I blindly search for another stick in a cotton pouch I keep at my bedside. I love the smell of the palo santo, but at this point, I pay far more attention to what I believe it is moving in my home on a cellular level.

When I think of fire's life span, one of the few and notable truths that I encounter is viability, an ability to survive successfully. Fire churns with little effort. It is also ravenous and, at times, untamable. The greetings I have with the little fires on the stick are almost always about a deal I'm making with it, one where I remain in control of its length, life span, and use. This kind of power comes with responsibility, as Dakota/Lakota Sioux writer Ruth Hopkins shares when explaining the use of sage, often employed to remove negative energy. "When using medicinal plants, it's important that the *plant is used sustainably*. When we pick sage, we always leave the root and say a prayer of thanks for our harvest. This is as much a part of smudging (or saging) as burning the plant is." The act of smudging has been appropriated by Westerners for years, with no acknowledgment of the historic illegality of it and ultimately, the genocide that often took place to do it. While some Indigenous people believe that sage shouldn't be sold at all, there are others who believe that if harvested sustainably, sold ethically, and burned intentionally and ceremonially with prayer, then non-Natives—and those of us who are bound to Native culture—can use it. Perhaps that is why I am slow to burn my own. Although my grandmother's father was Native, and we spent weeks and summers in his house and in his care, there are deep familial differences between my culture and Native culture. There is enough to call to be let in and not enough to call it mine.

The sage I keep lives on my grandmother's side table. It lies in a ceramic dish by my bed, remains hardly used, save after guests leave my home and nightmares don't leave my body. I purchased my first bundle of sage from a plant shop on Eleventh Street in the East Village, when I was in my early twenties and unaware of the ethics of purchasing. The local shop I use now gathers loads from a Native friend who sells them to her in large quantities rather infrequently. *Salvia apiana* (white sage) is a perennial desert shrub that grows several feet tall. Indigenous cultures have collected, dried, and burned it, using its smoke as medicine and in ceremonies, for centuries. Although this use of sage was necessary to Native culture, it was illegal in the United States until 1978, a way to erase the value and stories of their lives as a First Nation. Indigenous people still fight for the opportunity to perform their sacred ceremonies in hospitals and other locations, where their families may need the medicinal power of the burning sage at their bedsides, believing wholly and fully that this particular smoke heals all.

Sage smoke circles and swirls. It is massive and often swells sooner than I can release a prayer of thanks and/or forgiveness. Unlike the fire on a palo santo stick, sage will continue to burn out if left to its own devices. If finished to burn down completely, the sage only leaves remnants of its parts. Although no longer visibly recognizable, the debris left behind is pungent, and the twine used to wrap it remains nearly intact, ready to thread what was there and what remains.

"Anything you lookin' for in particular?" the man said to me at the hardware store a few blocks away from my apartment as I squinted and leaned over the counter, hoping to find what I needed without explanation.

"Yes, I'm looking for those stickers. For fires," I responded, apprehensive if he'd understand what I was talking about as I combed my memory for what they looked like exactly. "They're red. White, sometimes . . ." I recalled haphazardly.

"Oh, you mean the fire safety stickers that people stick on their windows?"

he offered. "I don't think we have them here. But they used to give them out at the fire department down the block. Maybe you'll have better luck there," he added as I walked out.

New York's fire season is a blip in the mind of a city dweller. It seems to happen without incident, without fanfare or an alarm to do something other than what we normally do. Except for people like me. People who haphazardly stroll through the swell of multiunit buildings on dry spring days and are alarmed by the faintest scent of backyard open burning, during our own fire season. There are laws in place that codify its existence. But if you're not paying attention, the only fire season you may know is the late-summer-through-fall soak out west. The kind that made the Fort Greene sky in Brooklyn a ripe peach one summer because of weeks on end of burning all the way across the coast. But the horror and truth out west do not diminish the silent truth of the east.

"We Are Okay!" read the white sign with rainbow letters, assorted stickers and handwriting that resembled a child's. The sign was taped to a door, the windows of the building were blown out, and black cascaded down the usual brown bricks of the brownstone. The side of the building was boarded up with untreated wood, and glass was shattered on the sidewalk and into the street. On the way to school, I hurried my children by, averting their eyes and shushing their questions with answers I didn't really have. Up in flames went their favorite pizza shop, and my son cried out about their summer ices that would be no longer. I thoughtlessly worried about my vintage coat in the dry cleaner's below—had the fur managed to survive? I put it in for a button fix the week before. It had to be on the first spindle behind the register. I concerned myself with the tenants, if they had money to stay somewhere else, and how okay was okay? After dropping the kids off at school, I stood at the corner where the building was and met a friend who was in tears. "I was fine until I read the sign," she said, attempting to swallow the knots in her throat.

After the conversation on the corner, where the sign made us pause, my hunt for the fire safety stickers resumed. But this time I searched the internet, where the results proved plentiful. The stickers available differed slightly from the ones I remembered as a child. Now they included white empty rectangles where you could write how many adults, children, and pets were in a home, so the fire department knew to save them all. I've not seen one in a window in years, but upon sight, I felt the sticker would bring me some kind of peace. Once in my cart, I started to imagine writing, "One adult. Two children. Two cats." To a burglar, it could signal that I was an easy target to ransack and assault. "One adult . . . check." To the police, who may come to my door one day, for no reason at all and every reason they could conceive, the sticker could signal to them that I am a Black woman—one adult, two children; the statistics of single parenthood meant I fit the profile—and they could easily fire bullets into my apartment while I slept, killing me, and call it justified. "Somebody kicked in the door . . ." One man, one twenty-six-year-old woman, a no-knock warrant, thirty-two shots, six landed, gunfire plumed at 3003 Springfield Drive, apartment 4. Breonna Taylor's life and death, like little fires, still visit me in my sleep.

After receiving my first Covid-19 vaccine dose, I could feel the drops of the small vial travel to my extremities. I qualified for an early dose because of a childhood diagnosis of lupus—which showed up at the same time as my vitiligo. Sitting in a large gray hall with plastic black folding chairs placed four feet away from one another, I settled in for my fifteen-minute post-vaccine waiting period to ensure there were no negative side effects. I watched as an elderly Black woman leaned in close to the neck of a National Guard member. I could tell that the last year of isolation had taken its toll, and the conversation was one of very few she'd had. Her stories wove around each other, filled with sparklers, life, and theatrics. But

the part that caught my ear was her insistence that she was "here for it all! The *fires and everything.*"

The fires she was speaking of, ones that swept across the Bronx years ago, impacted her and the city so much that she felt called to outline it all to some stranger. On the way home, overwhelmed with tears about standing on the side of the living (while nearly five hundred thousand others did not—those who were gone within minutes, days, and terrifying weeks in hospital beds, hallways, and their homes), I googled the city fires the woman so reverently discussed. I wanted to know who they swept up, and who they left behind to tell their stories.

Vivian Vázquez Irizarry was a kid in the 1970s during those Bronx fires the elderly woman mentioned. In her film, *Decade of Fire*, Irizarry highlights personal narratives from the community of people literally burned out of their homes— not just by landlords but by redlining, white flight, complex policies, and the closure of several fire stations. Several sections of the Bronx alone lost more than 97 percent of their buildings to fire and abandonment between 1970 and 1980. The film works to change the narrative of places like the South Bronx, and my home of Brooklyn, where generations of my family survived Crown Heights riots, displacement, blame, abandonment, and fires twenty years later, in the 1990s.

But when I think of fire ravaging land, I don't first think of these events. My mind travels even further back in time—to Tulsa in 1921, where, according to one observer, "the sidewalk was literally covered with burning turpentine balls" after a white-led massacre in the city left hundreds of Black residents dead; and back further still to the Red Summer of 1919, when in twenty-six cities across the United States, women and children were beaten and burned in their own communities by mobs of white men and women as Black people fought and begged for their lives. "It was not the union that brought this trouble; it was our crops," Alfred Banks shared with Ida B. Wells during her reporting of a 1920 massacre in Elaine, Arkansas. "They took everything I had."

Sometimes when I think of fire on land, I think of "Strange Fruit" and Black bodies swinging in the Southern breeze. I think of hundreds of years of fire used as a means of weaponization, unprovoked, and most often with the arsonist receiving no retribution.

"After a fire, your body has an inflammatory response. Your body reacts to that by shunting all blood and fluid to that area. But because your skin would normally hold in your body fluid, it leaks out everywhere," says Nicole Bernal, director of the UCI Health Regional Burn Center. After a brush with fire, adults have a far greater chance of survival than do the elderly and children. My obsession with the fire stickers led my research down a dark path wondering why folks set fires. More specifically, why some even set *themselves* on fire. I wondered how these awful realities informed how we talked about fire or even how we taught ourselves or our children about fire to begin with.

When I couldn't make peace (a cavernous fear that in my act to protect us, I'd place us at even more risk with burglars and the cops) with buying the stickers, I wrote out our fire plan in a journal. In the plan, the fires would always take place when we were sleeping. I'd touch my knob to see if it was hot; if it wasn't, I'd duck low and grab the kids from their room. We'd call for the cats, who would more than likely scratch at their door to be let out anyway. One by one, we'd crawl out the kids' window, with the cats zipped in backpacks, over the fence, and into our neighbors' yard. There, we'd have our neighbor call 911 while we found shelter in her home. If the knob was hot, I'd rip out my air conditioner unit with the force that only a mother in an emergency would have, exit my window, jump down (hoping not to break a limb), cross over, find the ladder I have hidden and accessible, pull down the kids' window, yell, "*Fire!*" to wake them up, and have them crawl out. In that case, I'd say nothing of the cats and pray we could retrieve them soon enough—which is the part of the plan you never share with children.

I learn by way of firsthand stories that help synthesize what I imagine and what I know to be practical. Fires are no exception. It was a sunny spring day in Brooklyn when I called Keia to talk about her apartment fire. The flowers had started to bud, and the yellow warblers and American woodcocks were singing their morning tunes, a stick of palo santo, a set of keys, and a book of matches next to me in a bowl my daughter, River, had made in ceramics class the year prior. I expected a story of tremendous loss, so I donned my armor. But it wasn't that way at all. My conversation with Keia taught me so much about my own nearly obsessive emotional and logistical fire journey after reading the "We Are Okay!" sign. On the call, I could hear her bangles clicking—as if they were symbols or clapping audience hands—between her words. Her slight Southern drawl peeked out every now and then, but I couldn't source from where or how long ago, and I didn't ask, because she said "Philadelphia," and that was enough.

During the afternoon we talked, the spring air in New York City felt eerie, as things were beginning to open after being shut down because of Covid for several months. In the background of our conversations stood the juxtaposition of everything being burned to bits with the respite that comes with a period of settling—knowing that artifacts, spirits, people (and their stories) not only outlive destruction but can celebrate in the aftermath.

It was June 22, 2016, and Keia had received an email. The fire had happened when she was at work as a "glorified executive assistant" in Germantown. "There's been a fire," the email read. "Here's the number for Red Cross. You can't come home."

Through bewildered laughter, Keia recounted what happened next:

> *I pack up from work and tell my bosses my house is on fire and I have to go. I pull up to the house in a penguin suit and flip-flops, and there are a bunch of guys there in lime-green fluorescent vests, vying for the job to be the first to board up the house.*

One of the guys gives me his vest, and he asks me, "What do you want to get?" I respond and say, "Grab as much as you can!" I had a bunch of things from my grandmother who passed away a few years prior, which I need. My apartment was destroyed, but not just because of the fire. It was because the fire department destroyed it trying to find the starter. They threw my couch through the window, and there was water inches high. Anything that was on the floor was waterlogged. The first thing I grabbed was a framed picture of my grandmother and my grandfather on their wedding day. It was the original photo, so I ran through the apartment with that clutched in my hand, collecting everything else. I'm not super religious, but I also grabbed the Bible my grandmother gave to me (she wrote in it at everything), which sat open on the coffee table, because that was the same way she had it when she was alive. The Bible cover was leather, the leather was wet, but the pages weren't. All of my other books were on my West Elm couch that was thrown on the side of the building. I kept clothes in my Ford Escape for weeks after that; my car smelled like a barbecue.

When Keia tells me about the clothes she wore on her way to her house from work, I see an image of my mother on 9/11. From her nine-to-five as a paralegal in Midtown, she walked under layers of ash and smoke with found flip-flops through downtown, across the Brooklyn Bridge into Prospect Heights. Keia doesn't have children, and it wasn't 9/11, but I kept striking the match, then blowing the fire out like some nervous tic.

Afterward, I stayed in a temporary apartment far from my job and spent so much time traveling just to work. During the day, I was busy enough to not worry. But at night, it hit me, and I would just cry for the entire night. Eventually, I moved in with my new boyfriend. My

landlord showed us design plans for the house (which was never built
back up) and tried to get all the tenants to sign a lease again to move
back in. But my boyfriend suggested that I stay. It was such a new
relationship, and I didn't want to live with a man again. But over time,
we renovated his house to be our house.

The fire was labeled undetermined, and I don't believe it. I lost so much.
But I realized that none of it really means anything, unless it was my
grandmother's. It still hurts. I have this beautiful relationship with this
beautiful man, and I am much more careful in what I bring in and what
I get rid of. And I am thankful for the fire because of that.

For Keia, the fire was less about what it took and more about what it gave
her. I heard the smile in her voice as she told me where her grandmother's stuff
remained in her house now. In a conversation with Krista Tippett, Dr. Bessel
van der Kolk, author of *The Body Keeps the Score*, shared:

> I think trauma really does confront you with the best and the worst.
> You see the horrendous things that people do to each other, but you
> also see resiliency, the power of love, the power of caring, the power
> of commitment, the power of commitment to oneself, the knowledge
> that there are things that are larger than our individual survival. And
> in some ways, I don't think you can appreciate the glory of life unless
> you also know the dark side of life.

I'm reminded here that in one of her interviews, filmmaker Vivian Vázquez
Irizarry shared that her favorite part of her documentary about the Bronx fires
was showing Puerto Rican and Black kids lying on their bellies on top of their
skateboards, riding freely down a street in the aftermath of the fires—the rubble
of the buildings behind them. She also noted the community gardens that took

shape soon after the fires as a response, and the birth of hip-hop that came shortly on its heels; music that saved millions of Black and Latino boys and girls, born from that same rubble.

When we heard a summer storm rolling into Clinton Hill on our run for another helping of ice, River counted the sounds of thunder. "Five minutes," she said curiously, with a hint of concern. The thunder grew louder, and I pulled the kids in close to my hips. They plugged their ears. The pace of their tiny toes picked up so we could miss the remaining rumbles and the soak of the cement. *Boom!* The thunder clashed again. "That one was closer! Two minutes!" she shouted, and we retreated, laughing and wailing at the storm to just hold off until we were safe in the apartment again. She learned her counting technique during a week spent with her grandparents in Maryland one summer. I imagine her grandfather wanted to quiet her midsummer storm fears and gave her a method to ease the anticipation of the inevitable. When I was young and a summer storm rolled by my grandmother's apartment in Prospect Heights, we didn't count the thunder or look at the way the lightning struck the sky. My grandmother shuffled us into a small room, protected by bedrooms in her railroad layout, turned out the lights, and explained how God was working. During those hours, it was better to be quiet and allow his tears to flow, his anger to flourish.

River and Oak aren't like me, though, and at home, questions of storms abound. I am not my grandmother, and religious tales don't really hold weight in my head, but I deliver a story anyway. When asked about flooding, I tell my children about Katrina and New Orleans, the images of elderly women standing on rooftops embedded in my diaspora. Although we do not know their names or their means of survival, as Black people, we have the burden and the honor of carrying them with us. Similarly to the way I sat in silence through the storms as a child—the world outside of Brooklyn corners mostly unknown to me—my children and I hold vigil for the world we absorb and the one we know exists beyond our vision. And sometimes, the one beyond our understanding.

I tell them of plastic orange lifeboats and men who carried the women out, floating couches and dining room tables; neighbors more reliable than the government we hold true. I tell them of Superstorm Sandy, when River was just a year old, that flooded homes and subways, and swept entire communities of low-income and poor Black people out from under the places they felt the most safe here in New York City. In those same breaths, I tell them of the hill we occupy in Clinton Hill, on Lenape land, which our ancestors built, and how it props us up from storms, leaving for later the terrible reality of the women and children who live at the bottom of it. I devote myself to preparing my children for storms they may never have to endure.

In the Oaxacan town of Teotitlán del Valle, women like Doña Viviana Alávez hold decades-old space for traditions while simultaneously unearthing and passing along the importance of breaking norms for future generations. In a profile for *Vogue*, at seventy-four, Doña Viviana speaks to writer Xóchitl Gonzalez through an interpreter about how the *velas tradicionales de concha* began as an ancient wedding tradition for brides and grooms who would "steal away" to get married. The *velas tradicionales de concha* is a colorful oval arch of waxed flowers in pink, green, and white, a thick beeswax center in its natural yellow hue that can reach up to five feet in length. Gonzalez describes the small Oaxacan village as smelling like sweet honey and wood. In the profile, Doña Viviana is photographed chopping a piece of wax purchased locally in Mexico with an axe half her size. Her wrinkled and strong fingers are pictured molding the petals of the candle and squeezing a lime to dye them naturally. The spindles where a dozen or more of the wicks hang look like the ones that sit in the back of my local dry cleaner, where my vintage coat once hung before the brownstone fire. Doña Viviana hoists herself up on an old wooden child's chair, then pours layers of wax as a coating to prepare the base for the *vela de concha*. The process is tedious and labor-intensive. It's not lost on me that the adornment of the *velas*, used as a barter to heal fractured relationships and families, is also seen as form of celebration. In my rapid American perception of the *velas tradicionales de concha*, I read the flower wreaths placed next to caskets as a last farewell. In this event, the flowers are the curtain call. The fire that awaits to be lit on the *velas de concha* is the convocation.

Dusty, vintage six-ounce mason jars with metal tops stand empty and ready near our stoop stairs as my children and I spot the first fireflies of our Brooklyn summer. River and Oak aren't afraid of how the fireflies feel in their dirty palms, as I once was as a kid. But the fireworks that begin as an entry and a celebration of summer still rile them up at almost seven and ten and a half. They begin on Memorial Day, a day my own family playfully calls the first day of "Black summer," when we begin to molt our worried skin. Fires are no longer banned in the city for fear of accidental ones. Rather, it is an apparatus used to wave folks in. Not only by way of the charcoal grill leaning in the back with an indistinguishable summer scent but by the early-evening run of fireworks that aren't only saved for July 4 around here.

There's this one photo I have of River as a baby in a pale pink wrap on my chest in the beginning of summer. She was no more than six months old, and in an act of new parent bravery and necessity, we skipped her bedtime to catch fireworks along the Hudson. Even though we were far enough so the sound wasn't too alarming, River funneled her head in the extra flap that was there to hold her close to my breast. I'm sure she could barely hear anything, but as the fireworks went off, she would occasionally wiggle her toes, pop her head out of the flap that also covered her ears, then retreat again. I'd look down, then tilt my head up at the night sky, only to return to her face. The photograph of us that evening is amusing because of what you don't see. I remember being terrified and confident in that way a new mother often is. I was finally out of the fog that consumes so many of us for months on end after labor. Things started to become clear. I knew what I was doing, but I also had no idea of the path ahead. Or at best, how I'd fare.

When the fireworks finished, I could faintly smell the sulfur in the air, and the onlookers disintegrated into large crowds, leaving behind the smoke and me to watch it settle. Fire carves its own path again and again, without our consent. When left with it, or with what remains after it, we find a series of things worth squeezing through the crack of hope. And if we are lucky, we get to commemorate whatever those things may be.

On the Line

Creating domestic bliss is especially useful for individuals living alone who are just learning to be self-loving. When we intentionally strive to make our homes places where we are ready to give and receive love, every object we place there enhances our well-being.

—BELL HOOKS

Before my kids, and sometimes before my work, the drying rack greets me. At times, it is simply the mental obligation: even in a pandemic, my kids have endless amounts of dirty clothes. At other times, it is the exchange for morning meditations, where I sit still with my legs crossed on the floor and count the deepest breaths out of my widening stomach. I choose a task that is a meditation of its own, a slow and religious act. The two-toned gray woven basket that I transport around my apartment every early morning for the laundry is carried slowly and steadily with my right hip cocked out, bearing its weight. The feeling is reminiscent of the way I used to carry each one of my babies. As such, when I move to do one thing with one hand, I hold on to the basket tightly with the other, being careful not to let it/them tilt or twist too much from one end to the next. On this particular day, it is the pull of twin cords that I hope helps wake up the room and me before 7:00 A.M. on a hazy and windy Brooklyn morning. When the shade rolls—folding one woven layer into the next with each tug—it reveals what's on the other side of my old iron-gated windows. The sun remains hidden by copious clouds, the vision of my neighbor's retired laundry line is my only wake-up call today.

My life on the line began soon after I was born during the scorching Brooklyn summer of '89. But my life *with* the line started after I had my daughter. I tried handwashing things when she was a few months old and we lived in a third-floor walk-up in Bushwick, Brooklyn. At first, it was just River's onesies and little T-shirts that pulsed with my hands in the sunken coated tub and tiny tin kitchen sink surrounded by particleboard. Years later, when I had Oak in a sublevel apartment in Clinton Hill, we purchased a baby-blue-and-white used portable washer that hooked up to the sink using a scrunchy-like tube to connect from one end to the next. When the clothes were finished with their wash, I climbed through our bedroom window, into a sunken six-foot-by-ten-foot drain, to hang the tiny laundry on a hemp rope, which we had originally used to cover our hot floor-to-ceiling radiator pipe in that same apartment. As I hung each little shirt and thick cotton sock, I mixed and matched the clothes, reminiscent of the laundry lines connecting other apartment windows throughout Brooklyn. More than that, they remind me of the multicolored plastic triangle flags that are often tied from the entry of a supermarket to the nearest lamppost, letting customers know that doors are open and shelves are hearty. These colors are a sign of life and, in a way, prosperity.

After that building was sold and we moved to a one-bedroom apartment (that we converted into two), we relied on a pickup laundry service, as time and landlord restrictions didn't allow for our washer hookup. In spite of that, I saved my underwear and bras for the tub and bathroom sink so I could get in deep and rub the edges of the linings together. Then I hung them up on doorknobs and other places wherever I saw fit. When considering those days, I often think of the Al-Anon saying, "It works if you work it."

In the fall of 2018, after moving again to a pre-war two-bedroom with a laundry unit in my apartment, I discovered that my dryer, which was left by my friend who occupied the apartment before I had, leaked into the basement below. It never dried anything particularly well, always taking a few spins, or seemed to only half steam a load of just-washed laundry. When removing the clothes, my fingertips would instantly get wrinkly—like a soggy, pale-brown sponge cake. I'd spring back from the piping heat, grabbing garments by the tips of collars or corner seams, with my index finger and thumb. Somehow, my laundry schedule seemed double that of my peers, and I repeated this act again and again. Getting another dryer was out of the question. The $700 I already spent on the washing machine to attach to this dryer had eaten enough of what I like to call "function funds"—a small pool of money that allowed repairs to take place without breaking my personal bank. When the dryer began to discharge through the nipple-shaped light fixture in the basement hallway, I was at once frustrated and relieved to no longer have to deal with a dying machine intent on scarring me with battle wounds.

Through the years, and through multiple apartments, possibly as a sign of an ongoing internal dialogue and longing, I held on to a six-foot double-stretched cotton line, hoping that one day I could string it across a larger back-yard of my own. Given my dying dryer, and the exorbitant cost to fix it, it seemed like now might be a good time to put the line to use. But the slab of concrete in my current backyard proved too large for the clothesline. One side of the brick to the other was awfully low, too. I searched for a pulley version instead that I could wrench on to the weathered wooden legs of an overhead covering that was mostly used for the rotating home junk my landlord tends to keep in the back-yard to send to her family in Haiti. While the laundry line could stand to be away from the rubble, overall, the optics just didn't make sense. And so, I abandoned my dream of the clothesline.

The drying rack I have now is plastic, with two winged sides that can fold in if I no longer need them. It doesn't hold tension in the same way the laundry lines outside do. You can't retire it by simply forgetting about its presence either. What I need, what my own line provides for me, is something that is solid; it can bear weight like nobody's business. It is beautiful, it is functional, and more im-portantly, it is reliable. It makes room for more. This laundry rack is like a piece of furniture, propping up and staying put when I see fit. And unlike furniture, when I am done with it, I fold it up, and the living room transforms into its for-mer self. The line allows me to care for the things I most desire in a way only my hands can do. If I hang garments too quickly, they run the risk of falling to the ground and getting dirty. At the same time, I realize that if I hang things deli-cately, they remain unsoiled and respectable. I am toeing the line almost always, delicately, intimately.

If I allow myself to dwell on these ideas more closely, I realize that my position on the line isn't settled only in that duality I feel when pulling my tucked-in rack from the side of the washing machine to stand erect and unfold under my sunny living room window. Or in the bliss-like melody I hear in my head while wringing, stretching, and placing our clothes on the line during a warm day. This feeling isn't *merely* a feeling. In a 2013 research essay, Dana Berthold makes these watery sentiments pellucid thoughts:

> We have all heard that cleanliness is next to godliness. The *Encyclopedia of Domestic Economy* stated in 1844 that "Cleanliness . . . has moral as well as physical advantages . . . it is an emblem, if not a characteristic, of purity of thought and propriety of conduct" (Heneghan 2003, 133) . . . In its purposive distancing from the laborer who is conceived as dark and dirty, a dirt-free hygienic aesthetic confers higher status, partly because it is expensive. Some might argue that cleanliness is an aesthetic having much more to do with class than with race. But we can see from the history of these ideals that the two have been inseparable in America.

At any given time, the laundry on my rack is an ostentatious blend of old things and new things. Hardly ever is the light white. And hardly ever am I not drawn to the humming belief that if my clothes were white, maybe I wouldn't worry so much if they were actually clean? I would see it so clearly. So much so that my own clarity would be extended out and into the world, and narrate ahead of me, how I was possibly perceived by others as well. At the same time, I realize while hanging my things that I am not the commodified white stay-at-home mother with the wooden rack propped in her photographable kitchen. Nor am I the sole laborer, pinching coins and laundering to make ends meet. I have never thought of myself as a gymnast, but the experience of tiptoeing, leaning into, and tangling with these ideas has convinced me otherwise. I belong with those who so often find themselves in the middle—fighting with the narrative of femininity, purity, and domesticity within the arch of generations of women holding that often taut, stretched, and old line as well.

A clothesline should be able to support the weight of two loads of wet clothes on a sunny day. That's about thirty-five pounds of shirts, pants, and undergarments. If the line sags too much, a metal prop at the center can balance the weight of the line to keep its performance the same. Fail to prop the line and the clothes will scrape the ground—but even then, as they dry, they lighten and lift, rising toward the sun, as if the whole line exhaled. In the city, the lines looped across from apartment window to apartment window can be read as a distinct class marker. Those who happen to use a line may be incorrectly read as caring nothing of the environment or the longevity of their clothes, only using the line as a result of the class system they inhabit. As laborers themselves, they return home only to labor some more, with far less than those they serve. In several black-and-white photographs spanning from the early 1900s to the late 1950s, shot in Brooklyn, Thompson Street, Greenwich Village, and way up into Harlem, photographers documented the life of the line in the city. Lissa Rivera describes the archive of photos of clothes on the line as a sort of census for the city, that alludes to "bodies not present." Rivera goes on to describe "the clothes-lines as a visual element in depictions of poor and working-class neighborhoods. It often added physicality to the frame, serving as a system of measurement of overwhelming heights. Each diagonal line became a symbol of the chaos and intersection of lives and cultures within an imposed vertical grid. The clothing was a recurring character of universal need."

As the pandemic descended upon New York City, the word *ventilator* became one spoken so often, I found myself lying in bed on sky-blue air-dried sheets, staring at the ceiling, performing a repetition of its syllables like I was counting little fluffy sheep, hoping the exercise might help me drift off. *Ven-*

ti-la-tor. Lying on top of my linens, the only struggle for breath I experienced was the anxiety of invisible sickness that was in the air, on our shoes, all over our hands, and even, maybe, in our sheets, pressed atop my chest like a stack of bricks, daring to let me sleep. The space between the well and unwell was so slim, and all we needed was a *ventilator.*

In June of 1892, the same year Ellis Island opened at the mouth of the Hudson, George T. Sampson, a Black man, patented one of a few solutions, if you will, to the labor of the line. While Europe had been working on what we now know as a dryer for some time, Sampson had reconsidered the risk and reward in making something safer and far more efficient. His invention, known then as a *ventilator,* suspended a frame that would allow the clothes to be dried by the heat of the stove, without them smelling, or worse, causing the garments to burn up in flames. And much like the drying rack I use over a century later, it could be like a piece of furniture, put away when not in use. Sampson is hard to find in our catalog of history, though. In my research, I find little of anything about his accomplishments. Instead, Sampson becomes a bridge, a thread of many in the cord.

Ventilation is defined as the movement of air between our lungs and the oxygen we breathe upon exhalation and inhalation. The *respiratory system* requires six vital processes of gas exchange: the airway, lungs, chest wall, respiratory muscles, phrenic nerve, and *respiratory center.* In my apartment, the reminder to not only let my body breathe but to give the room its breath often arrives in the lifting of the window—the system that allows the outside air in, as an effort to evenly dry and oxygenate the clothes and people on the line is simple in a world that is not so.

On the cover of *Vogue,* in the summer of 2018, Beyoncé stood tall and erect in a gown that displayed the colors of the Pan-African flag in front of a clothesline on a sunny day in a field of green. In the photo, instead of items hanging on the clothesline, Beyoncé held a white sheet in both her hands. It blew back in the wind, almost as if it were a parachute ready to carry her away. Later, in a series of Instagram stories, Professor Elissa Weichbrodt assessed that Beyoncé's cover pushed the perceived boundaries on Black femininity and labor, power, womanhood, fabulosity, and causality. She was holding her own sheet *in front of the line*, dressed to the nines, shaking up the narrative. Beyoncé was, in that issue, the most candid she has ever been, detailing the complexity of racism, maternal health, and mortality, and this strange juxtaposition of being in power and, at once, slipping without consent or full awareness, into the role of victim. What struck me then—and strikes me still—is how one of the most dynamically talented women in the entire world, who had just given birth to twins, felt the need to make this big declaration of an internal debate not only of identity but of the impossible road of racism and how it seeps into the grandest experiences (birth and performance) as well as the most minute (dressing and cleaning). Certainly, Beyoncé isn't doing the labor of her own laundry. But in the quiet corners of our lives as Black women, despite her own closeness to capitalism and her ability to be so rich—to be *other*—I believe Beyoncé's position in that article aims to show that the line from her to me, or me to you, is so very thin in the eye of whoever holds us at any given moment. Stand in front of the line. Hold the line. Throw it over the line. Do what you may, but what we struggle with internally is in constant step with a larger, historical, complex discussion about Who We Are.

Beyoncé's *Vogue* cover invokes the legacy of the Black washerwomen, who went on strike in Atlanta during the summer of 1881. It was these women who were the start of that bridge to Sampson and his ventilator. These washerwomen were sole providers for their homes, a decade after their emancipation. What began as a twenty-person movement for better wages and respect for their labor—an increasingly necessary commodity—ballooned to a group of three thousand. In the task of laundering clothes for wages, choosing their own hours, and deciding on their own amount of work, Black women created a system in which their bodies and abilities were needed for the demanding and often multi-tasking position that wasn't appealing or worthwhile to even poor white women in the South. The duality of this breadwinning work in contrast to the honor and softness that comes with performing your own labor is something I'm familiar with generations later.

The garments were heavy. Black women made their own detergent out of lye and used beer barrels cut in half for their washing tubs. They often worked out of their homes, their children at their feet. When the garments were ready to dry, the washerwomen didn't use measly folding racks; they thrust their arms, pushed their hands, and threw the weighted clothes over laundry lines, while pressing the pieces that dried with massive industrial irons. Those same hands and arms that made their own detergents out of need unconsciously taught women like me, knowledge passed through generations, to pick the vinegar over the Woolite and to always set panties and bras to Hand Wash or Delicate in the washing machine (although true handwashing is always the best choice).

Those same women believed that activism was one of their most important tasks. They knocked on doors in their community to inform people of their strike and also to gather other Black and white women laborers alike. In newspaper clippings from those years, journalists sympathized with white families whose clothes arrived back to them "wringing wet" as the washerwomen went on strike. These same journalists accused the washerwomen of abusive antics, disorderly conduct, and other accounts of aggression, for which they were jailed, then released and fined. Possibly, this is one of the earliest examples of a Black woman being labeled as angry if she speaks up for herself, no matter how just her response. In one of only a few documentations of their own of this fight, the washerwomen wrote to Atlanta's then mayor, James English, stating: "We can afford to pay these licenses, and will do it before we will be defeated, and then we will have full control of the city's washing at our own prices, as the city has control of our husbands' work at their prices." In the meantime, the laundry piled up, and the white families who relied on the washerwomen's work eventually folded. The Black women won. They didn't just win the right of decent wages for tenuous labor; they won the right to have their labor honored and valued by not only their white clients or the local government but also *themselves.*

I imagine that strikes like these laid the groundwork for the Great Migration, which I am certain my own maternal great-great-grandmother was part of as she made her way from North Carolina to New York. In New York, with the promise of better jobs and wages, she eventually had my great-grandmother, my great-grandmother had my grandma, my grandmother gave birth to my mother, and there, on shared generational blocks in Brooklyn, my mother had me. I remember all of these women at once, a rarity only given by the grace of youthful birthing and tenacious souls. I remember their work, their homes, their spirits; and I imagine their unwavering and steady hands as a kaleidoscope of various laborers in their own right, de-layering generation by generation, so that somehow, like the women who came decades before I did, I may return to the comfort of my home, during hours of my own making, to work and launder my own clothes and raise my own children.

I don't recall a laundry line in my childhood, no tight rope or cotton braid on which my mother hung our things. Cleaning was, still, a requirement of life. Like in most Black households, it was done on Sunday. It started for my mother at the crack of dawn, with a song and an idea of what to cook for the evening, and so the kitchen was likely up first. We kids woke early, too—ate, then began our day sorting our messes, folding our clothes, wiping down everything in sight. We didn't just stick to our bedrooms; we also swept through the living room, dining room, and bathrooms alike. When it was all said and done, the music had lowered and the sun was deeply setting behind its own corner of the world. The objects, clothes, and dust that had accumulated in my mother's room during the week was ours to sort through and pick up as well. She was tired by then. It was our job, we understood, and while this fact was often frustrating, it was also, somehow, a pleasant delight.

During the week, my mother worked a nine-to-five in a law office under pressures and what I now understand as racist structures. She clerically cleaned up the messes of rich people, simultaneously playing referee via telephone for the arguments and disastrous messes her children caused throughout the day. I can't remember how many times I called my mother at her office from our kitchen phone asking some question or wanting her to fix some brawl that I had with my siblings or at school. Even when she was at the office, she was still with us. And when she was with us, she was very much there. No matter the time or location. When my mother reentered our home from the day, tired, with black pumps clutched in her hand and sneakers on her feet, a clean house was the one gift we were supposed to give her. "I want it how I left it," she would say. Imagine that as a single simple request in life—*Leave it as I left it.*

Black women have always been fastidious. Somewhere between slaves, washerwomen, doctors, lawyers, and writers, there's a thread about how society sowed a perception and tradition. In her essay, Dana Berthold, for lack of a better phrase, cleans this up:

> People of color . . . sometimes manifest this concern, perhaps precisely because they have been systematically denied class mobility (while simultaneously being told to clean up their act and pull themselves up by their bootstraps) . . .
>
> For whites, this anxiety is rooted in an actual historical concern to protect one's class position by guarding against racialized "taint" . . . To form a legitimating discourse, it has been important for whites to believe a contradiction: that it was non-whites' own fault if they

didn't "clean" themselves up . . . *and* they were objectively unable to be clean, because they were irrevocably tainted.

Cleanliness, being next to godliness, includes a perverted version of morality. Our bodies were never clean enough, but desired for the service of others. Our homes, never good enough, until they were taken away and used for someone else's land. Our ideas not skilled enough, until co-opted and rebranded by others. Pumping through the veins of generations of Black women is the understanding that we could be judged for anything and everything, at any minute, and also have that judgment leveled against us. It is like having a dream: you begin to feel as if you're falling out of a tree, but instead of ever hitting the ground, you wake up in the middle of the night, hot and sweaty with an iron-stiff back. Our bodies, our habits, our ideas belong to us, and they are a reminder of what doesn't belong to us. We are creators, and we are reactions, centuries'-old answers to *what to do when.*

By contrast, I am mystified by unkempt homes, the kind where dishes stack to form towers on the counters, where toys, shoes, books, laundry—*things*—live comfortably underfoot. The one time I can remember my home being messy was when I was first living on my own, and I spent a lot of time running away from my home and myself. My clothes were medicinal remedies for my loneliness. Coincidently, in the absence of real people, I soon found out that I spent a good portion of my tenure in that apartment unknowingly forming tiny organs and sprouts of toes in my uterus, where my one-day daughter found a warm place to call home for ten full months.

Growing a home *for her,* I learned to grow my own, to answer my own questions about where to keep the mop and broom or what oil to burn to get that scent or how much I should be paying in rent. I learned to set boundaries, escaping those "I'm just outside your front door" drop-ins and asking for a text or a call as a heads-up. This was a truth I developed within my own space, to understand resistance. To choose to have things tidy or not. To choose to welcome a guest or not. To relieve myself of imposition. To be a Black woman, who, honoring our history, valued the sanctity of being especially prepared for guests—the way we always are in service to others and their needs. When I think about my messy apartment back then and my decision to build an orderly home with rules now, my mother's words come back to me: "You always have to treat your home as if guests will arrive."

Although I had children, a family, and a host of friends, very rarely did my mother's proverb come to fruition. As a perpetual host of parties, for every reason and no reason at all, I have friends pop by briefly, on their way out someplace or taking a moment to pull me away from my own flickering blue screen; but they always ask first, to make sure I'm home or to make sure they're not interrupting something. They don't just show up, and they surely don't expect a sudden invitation in.

That was until the first summer of the pandemic, when people hardly saw one another, let alone entered the homes of their comrades. But on a wonderful warm Saturday, when I decided to leave the chaos of my home and my head for a day of gallivanting around Clinton Hill and Fort Greene with River and Oak, things changed. Roaming, drinking wine, having conversations, kids playing with sticks, and the unwillingness of letting the day end meant our miniature party of a few friends and neighbors lingered on our stoop—which at first didn't feel like anything at all, until I was asked a question: "Can I use your bathroom?" There was a little jiggle and a shake to signify the emergency of it. It took everything in me to not say, "No. Don't you live close by?" It wasn't just the contagion levels, germs finding their way into my home in spite of homemade cotton masks, or onboard unclean fingers pressed against my blue wallpaper. It was actually more about how I left our home that morning, ignoring it for the call of the warm weather and day out with my kids. It was what I left, knowing that it was Saturday and tomorrow was Sunday, when we would then pour our energy and arm strength into sweeping, wiping, and hanging our lives back in order. It was what I left, knowing that it was *ours* to leave, and I felt safe in that. "Sure," I said simply. After I fumbled with the key, I pointed straight down the hall, evading all other parts that she surely didn't have to see. She didn't get lost. But on her way back outside, whether she meant to or not, casually and unaware, she let me know she'd *seen*. "It's so good to know that your house is just like ours," she declared, tiptoeing back onto the stoop. "It always seems so neat and clean in photos."

All those years, my mother had been preparing me for a moment like this, a moment that would crystallize itself into our folklore, joining her stories, my grandmother's stories, my great-grandmother's stories. They were stories that told us why we do what we do, why we are who we are—a sense of identity that would be inherent no matter how many of my own boundaries I chose to create. Whether my apartment was truly messy that afternoon is neither here nor there. The issue isn't even in that she asked to use the bathroom or that I let her. The issue is in the stitch of that cord, that for most people is so very passive it is hard to see. But the stitch stays woven nonetheless. With a single comment and a swift exit, she unconsciously ventured past the physical spaces in my home of which I allowed, to bring me down somewhere deep and ordinarily armored with the clothes found on the line. There is no amount of affirmation or taking stock of what actually exists that erases that kind of deep-seated ping. The kind that knocks you directly off your perch and is presented to remind you of where you truly stand in this proverbial caste system. For better or for worse, my mother's voice, backed by a choir of our ancestors, confirmed my notions of this tug-of-war in my own Black cleanliness, both as my heritage and as my charge, always up for second-guessing and reminding.

One of the more generous gifts I've given myself, one that was complicated and perpetuated by all of this, is that of my very own domestic help: a house cleaner who arrives at my front door every other week. (When the stoop incident occurred, it was my house cleaner's week off.) Even when she would come, I still performed my Sunday clean, dressing my apartment for her date. It took me years to admit that I needed someone else's hands to help me clean and just as long for it to feel normal. I have lived and worked out of the same space since the beginning of my family, and this strains the bones of a home in a peculiar way. The labor of work and the work of a family is all completed within the same four walls of my house, as if my homelife and my life outside home each require all the hours of my days. This is not an unusual issue for households, particularly for women in the United States, where we are fighting against both government policy *and* ourselves. There are organizations, like the National Domestic Workers Alliance, which I have supported and held in considerable regard for some time, that fight for this struggle. The National Domestic Workers Alliance's work, including their "Fight for $15," was built under the legacy of those Black washerwomen who demanded dignity and fair wages fewer than two centuries ago. What used to feel like a secret—a strange affair with cash left next to the keys on the table—is now like a partnership that feels sacred. We call each other *Ms.* We ask about the kids. We talk about the weather. And, perhaps most routinely, she requests that I not worry.

I hardly ever fold clothes as I remove them from the line. I return to them sometime later in the evening, with a show and a glass of wine, making the task itself an opportunity to unwind. I don't find the act of folding as meditative as running the laundry, but it's there, in practice. Then one day, without question, notice, or pause, my house cleaner began to fold the clean laundry I had left sitting in white wire baskets next to my bed—the sleeves of sweaters crossed, hoods tucked in, underwear and socks bundled. Unmatched socks were left neatly on the side corner of the basket, ready to be placed in an old off-white cotton shoe bag hanging on the doorknob in my children's room. But we share something far more intimate that I think laid the groundwork for this kind of care, that enveloped its sanctity: life as caretaking women of color. In my case in particular, life as a Black woman.

Around the same time my house cleaner began folding my clothes, I read bell hooks's *All About Love* as a map and regenerative task on truly loving myself and those in my life and community. In relation to my house cleaner and the bigger picture that stood between and all around us, I continued to think of hooks's theory of a *love ethic,* in which she asserts, "We must collectively return to a radical political vision of social change rooted in a love ethic and seek once again to convert masses of people, Black and nonblack. A culture of domination is anti-love. It requires violence to sustain itself. To choose love is to go against the prevailing values of the culture." bell hooks uses Peck's words to further this process: "I therefore conclude that the desire to love is not itself love. Love is as love does. Love is an act of will—namely both an intention and an action. Will also implies choice. We do not have to love. We choose to love."

Based on a moral compass—or, quite possibly, love—I know that when my house cleaner changes from her outside hijab into her inside head covering, I scurry like a roach in particleboard. I leave the cleaning supplies out, and I ask her about *her.* I apologize if I am in the way and help take the bags to the garbage when she's ready to leave as I catch her gathering them. I say thank you, as many Americans do, in tips as well. And, like she told me not to worry, I decided not to be embarrassed by the questionable life span of my underwear, neatly folded, no matter how threadbare. I believe my house cleaner helped lay the ground of this kind of love ethic alongside me, where neither one of us, despite the fact that I pay her, could claim any sort of dominance. I did not stand in judgment of her for her position. And she did not stand in judgment of me for mine. Together, we built this space. A space in which I was not ashamed by her generosity in folding my clothes without being asked. I decided not to ever make mention of it, as it felt like a tear in something precious.

There are plenty of ways to wash dirty clothes. You don't need a house cleaner or a standard washing machine. When I was a child, we washed plenty of our intimates and basics in sinks full of sudsy water, a regimen my son has taken to when washing his favorite T-shirt: run the water until the sink is halfway full, pour in a little detergent, drain the water, use cold water to rinse, wring, and hang it on the line or the radiator of your choosing—which goes to show, you don't need a dryer either. Central heating or a radiator does the work of a conventional dryer, with less environmental harm.

Perhaps the task of placing my children's pants on the rack along with my woolen sweaters and tired jeans is my own kind of therapy. The slow method of wringing a garment over the sink, the act of stretching it over the stacked cylinders that connect the racks' wings. Watching a sunny Brooklyn day pass in the process—how the three o'clock hour illuminates an apartment's floating dust bunnies and speckled sun patches just so; how an open window can let in the vibrant scents of rosemary, eucalyptus, or thyme, no matter the season. An old lead-based radiator's steam whistles a little song that ultimately allows the slow inner warmth on the hem of the garments to become a tactile experience.

I am a washerwoman, working and making my home on my way home to myself. I do this the way I know how, the way I see fit, with generations of other women behind and in front of me. There are those who are beside me, too, that resist, pull, walk, work, sing, labor, use, convene, and find their joy on and with the line, ready to give and receive as we always will.

For Colored Girls Who Sang in the Kitchen When Time Hushed

i survive on intimacy & tomorrow

—NTOZAKE SHANGE

n my grandmother's north Brooklyn kitchen, there was a two-burner hot plate placed over a golden brown front-load dryer. Her oven worked. Her stove did not. There was a retro freezer that filled with frost, as well as a dining table that had to be nearly six feet long in the center of the room-like kitchen, leaving only enough space for us to carefully walk around it. There were times when my family packed that kitchen, around the table, rotating spots and stories while my grandmother cooked or sat briefly at the table to do some activity.

My grandmother's helpings were savory, routine, and meager, due in part to her disdain of waste. She had raised four children on a shoestring budget, and Brooklyn life was increasingly expensive for her (even in the '90s and in a rent-controlled apartment). She was a specific cook. She was routined. We were often served two tiny fried chicken wings and a baby bowl of her signature spaghetti. The bags of chicken had to be the same brand at all times. The sauce for the spaghetti was never a compromise.

It was easy to move from her kitchen to the hallway, almost as if they were living rooms, too. I spent entire summers sitting on the top step of her building's dimly lit staircase with a tin box filled with crayons as she taught me the art of coloring inside the lines. It was something she did when she wasn't recording the Sunday minutes, thrifting, or getting dressed just for the heck of it. We made pictures of Cinderella, Sleeping Beauty, Moses, Adam and Eve, always in varying shades of brown, with a thick, darker brown shade outlining their bodies and features. "Hang it up right there!" she'd demand while pointing to a spot on her refrigerator. "Make sure you sign your name, too." Each of the pictures she drew had her name in cursive written with crayon in the bottom right-hand corner: *Bertha.* Although my pictures were not nearly as neat as hers, her request that I make art and then display it in one of the most sacred spaces in her apartment was a gift. In that Prospect Heights kitchen, my grandmother taught me that what we did not see, we imagined. And what we did not have, we created.

On the south side of Richmond, Virginia, on a dead-end street, there is a house with a two-season sunroom, an oversize porch, and a mother's suite over the garage. Inside this house, in my grandmother's mother's kitchen (we called her Mommy), she had a cornered TV you could watch from any angle and that used to play soap operas all day long: *Days of Our Lives, The Young and the Restless, All My Children*. Despite taking up most of the kitchen, the plain dining table faded into the background almost always, but especially when Mommy was sitting at it—with rotating place mats and Coca-Cola-colored accents like a bread box and an ice pitcher. She loved to show off. At her table, she was not only happy, she was empowered.

Mommy's kitchen had an electric stove she knew how to work *like so,* an ice machine that always over-delivered into twelve-ounce white Styrofoam cups. And a sink with a window that looked out to the porch. Most of the family gathered at her house at least once a year for tables piled with Southern soul food: barbecue, black-eyed peas, chicken, cornbread, rice, baked macaroni and cheese, pigs' feet, and a side salad thrown together from a bag with sliced carrots and cucumbers tossed in. There was always so much food, and Mommy would wrap full paper plates in tinfoil, forcing us to take the leftovers home. She also worried about wasting, but her approach was different from my grandmother's. Mommy had an extra freezer in her mudroom and one in her garage, and also frequented discount grocers and food kitchens.

When the kitchen table couldn't fit all the guests at any given gathering, we spilled onto the porch, where six more could be seated. And when that eventually became too crowded, we flowed into lawn chairs on her land and then into her garage with little foldable tables doing the trick in front of the big-screen TV she'd set up there. Mommy, who outlived her daughter, my grandmother, was active and vibrant well into her eighties—she still drove and traveled, loved to gossip on the phone and cook her meals. She knew, intimately, a sense of freedom and abandon—and displayed it most notably in that kitchen, in that house she owned.

Food as language has been reinvented in my family over generations. It seems as if each of the matriarchs that preceded me had their own path of providing sustenance to those they know and love. My grandmother cared for her children, her grandchildren, and the friends of my uncle and aunt, who found refuge in her apartment and around her table, but also historically, for the students at the local public school where she assisted and substituted. Mommy spent much of her life caring for her grandchildren, foster children (official and unofficial), and the children of the white families who she nannied. I never met a single one of those families, but I heard about them as near characters. "Those white people loooooveeee me!" she would say, giggling. "I still get letters!" she would recall whenever a conversation ebbed to white-versus-colored-folk categories, which was customary for the Southern side of my family.

"What's for dinner?" my children ask as they walk home from school. A question I didn't dare ask or assume I would be told at their age. Not only out of fear of being perceived as nosy but because the security of dinner was something I never questioned. It's possible I give my children more of a reason to wonder. Or maybe it is just a sign of the times. "Gentle parenting, my butt," I'm sure Mommy would say if she were still alive. My path of seeing my children and of feeding them remains entirely different from how my maternal ancestors approached these things, but I am infused with their ways nonetheless. Annie's mac and cheese is usually dinner on a school night. But there is no chicken or pigs' feet in my kitchen—we are vegetarians. White rice, couscous, quesadillas, and beans. Kale and Beyond Meat sausage replace collards and turkey neck. I bake quiches and blueberry pies instead of candied yams, and River hates red sauce, so there is no Rao's. Pasta night is sautéed eggplant, squash, marinated onions, and peppers.

My grandmother and her mother loved being busy, but also generously feeding the stomachs and the souls of others. As if their bodies couldn't stop even if they tried. Maybe as if Black women, specifically, have always done this. I don't do the feeding part so easily. But busy is practically embodied in my genome. It is mainly because of those women before me that I care for my children in the way that I do, constantly hosting the kids of friends, finding weekly reasons to congregate with people I love, having large annual parties where everyone can flow in and out of our apartment. It's also why I tell stories and write them.

My grandmother's kitchen synthesized her different parts; her personality and her work as a community activist, her role as the wife of an artist, and as a fashion maven. Her kitchen gave the sense of all that she was. It was a museum, and she was its curator, director, docent, designer, and historian. At no more than five feet tall, she would reach beyond her dryer with the hot plate above it, into a three-foot-high cubby that stood behind it, where she kept a quintessential laundry cart and hundreds of multicolored recycled plastic bags folded into one another, then another. And those bags sat inside oversize red, white, and blue bags with top zippers I'm almost certain she purchased from Conway. On the kitchen table, my grandmother stocked faux fruit and vegetables of various colors: onions, apples, oranges, and purple grapes. They were coated in lacquer and so shiny you wanted to gnaw on them, to get to the sweet fruit that you knew just had to be underneath. And akin to museums with their white, four-inch-by-six-inch description plaques, if you simply asked, my grandmother would tell you the how, why, and where of everything in that room and beyond it. *Hint:* You did not need more kitchen tools, a more eclectic menu, fatter pockets, or even a fully functioning stove.

In the kitchens of both of these women, my grandmother and my great-grandmother, I learned the absolute.

. . .

"This is Heaven 1580!" I'd hear a man sing through a staticky line on my grand-mother's radio. It sat next to her window overlooking the overgrown backyard three stories down. Heaven 1580 was an AM station that had evolved over the years. Hosts were cult-followed, and in a 2001 article in *The Washington Post, Joy in the Morning* hosts Cheryl Jackson and Matt Anderson likened their time on the air to a way to get listeners to choose God anytime and anywhere of the day. "There's no reason for us to be old and tired. This is not yo' grandmama's gospel no more," Jackson jokingly said. "We love Grandma, but we want Grandma to go along with us for the ride." Oh, how my grandmother was along for the ride.

Whenever the line dropped or got fuzzy, she moved the antenna around to make it a little clearer. When it was clear, I could hear the preaching and the announcements floating out of the kitchen to the fire escape and back out to the top of the hallway steps on which I sat. The radio was the constant backdrop to the abundant scenes that took place under that kitchen chandelier. What I found fascinating then, as I do now, is that it didn't matter that the music was gospel or if it was in the middle of a service it was broadcasting—my grandmother would frequently pause with a wooden spatula in her hand and exclaim to us kids: "Come on! Do the bump!" A calf-length white lace skirt moved with her hips, and a dainty white cotton button top she'd washed in the tub next to the kitchen adorned her upper half. "Come onnnnn!" she would sing. Soon enough, my siblings and I would jump from our mahogany seats at her table and tap our hips together with hers as we snickered through the moves and the cooking.

"Dance with me!" I demand, stretching out my left hand to Oak. He grabs it with his right and spins under my arm. Dinner is Sade, Anita, or Nina. "Young, gifted, and Black is where it's at," they sing as Oak's half smile reveals reluc-tant joy. He is sensitive. Gentle. Always intimate and tender in the way I hope boys will be. At times, I've propped up my phone in a small pocket in the cutting board that is made for scanning recipes on the phone, using it instead to browse through our music. Oak dips his body onto my left arm, pushes his chest out, leans his curls into my hips. We sway together, and I laugh, my lips buckling above my teeth. The shape of his body moving along to a beat with mine eases my weary heart when I am sad or, worse, lonely, in the way words cannot articulate. In these moments, I think of those two women, who Oak never had the chance to know, but who may have dreamed of him the way my mother did when he remained in my belly as I prayed for his safe arrival from their side to mine.

The summer before her eleventh birthday, my daughter ripened with wisdom, sucked teeth, zealous conversations, and a fervor that tempts waters far deeper than I traverse. Her body bore buds: pomegranate lungs, string bean legs, and plums germinated from her chest. When I waddled under the dusty J train in Bushwick with her inside my newly womanly body, everyone asked if I was ready. "You look ready!" they would proclaim, gesturing to the girth of my growth. I wasn't sure if I was then. I am certain—as this young lady, a someday woman, appears before me at my kitchen table in meticulously laid black eyeliner—that I was ready then, and I am still ready now. I offer River what I can; she takes what pleases her.

On lingering afternoons when River was an infant she sat in a baby swing across the room in our railroad apartment, a glass round-edge dining room table my mother gifted me from her old apartment separating us. On the table, a roaring bouquet of flowers and small knickknacks. River cooed and blabbed as I shook the cabinets to find the duck sauce behind the peanut butter. The laminate flooring made me slide around in my socks, while River delighted in the nursery rhyme music playing from my phone. I could faintly smell the *arroz con gandules* and *sofrito* dribbling between the door hinges from my Puerto Rican neighbors as they moved between apartments and swapped dishes like some pastel-colored commune.

I stopped eating pork when I was eleven, so I mastered chicken and turkey. It was my grandmother's sweet-and-sour chicken that I came to learn to cook after I had River. I was planning my wedding on a part-time sales associate and pizza guy's budget, and ordered Chinese food from down the block every other day to sustain me. I scooped rice into my mouth above her bobbing nursing head. My grandmother collected duck sauce from the local Chinese restaurants that knew her by her first name. Packets filled tchotchke bowls that sat on her old chestnut table. She snipped them delicately with gold shears she had hidden in a drawer next to her hot plate. I searched aisles at the local supermarket for large tubs with my baby strapped to my chest. I banged the black tin caps on the laminate countertop to prop them open, and calculated how well this worked for our meager food budget. When the chicken was done, I sat at that table with my baby, delighting in what I had created. My time in the kitchen then was as much about growing up and learning as a new young mother as it was about patching tattered holes via that recipe for the women we were then and the women I hoped we'd become.

The apple River now slices across the bamboo board at the marble bistro table is cut in perfect widths. I hang back and ask that she move carefully. "I am, Mommy! I know!" She has learned her way around our kitchen. A pale yellow oil-stained recipe book sits at our counter between the other cookbooks, and lately, she flips through it to create something of her own making and on her own time, without my assistance. Lemonade becomes strawberry lemonade in the afternoon. She cracks brown eggs and toasts whole wheat bread on non-stick pans with her brother perched atop a step stool when I am still sleeping, only to bring french toast to my bedside for me when I wake. Grilled cheese, oatmeal, omelets, avocado toast, a salad or two or three she does so well.

Many mornings before River walks in with her full face, ready to cook, while I'm still threading together my words, I wonder about what we're creating at that marble kitchen table. The connection is slow, much like the purchase of the table itself. I reluctantly bought it from Wayfair after searching for months on end for one that had decades lacquered to its iron legs. In the end, I chose what was not only cheapest but easiest, one that could withstand kids' scratches and my own early-morning coffee stains. The table had no story of its own, but I placed it under our kitchen window with a beige-and-orange scarf as a curtain, a Japanese paper lantern hanging above it. When River enters, I turn off my morning BBC playing from the fridge and switch to "Three Little Birds" by Bob Marley. At times, she'll catch me ingesting a few Instagram videos. "Because it's my business!" Tabitha Brown's Southern drawl cheers from the square screen as River sits down. In her midforties, Tabitha has an approach to family, faith, womanhood, veganism, and cooking that has engrossed me. She's transparent and self-reflective—the follower recognizes immediately just how busy and grounded she is. Tabitha alone has supported my own upheaval of how women in the kitchen are supposed to look and act—and what they're supposed to create.

In Tab's world, she cooks and records meals herself. When each video nears its end, she sits at her dining room table with one hand holding a fork, and the other the phone, and says, "Oooh, God, we thank *you* for this food," and proceeds to eat with as much personality as she cooked with. Her delight is audible. And for the most part, the meals are incredibly easy. Although Auntie Tab (as many of us like to think of her) has manifested her stardom since her high school days, for those of us who don't know her intimately, it seems as if in a few short years Tabitha has become a multi-hyphenated maven. She's written books, acted, hosted a children's show called *Tab Time* (for which she was nominated for an Emmy), became an investor in companies that promote wellness, created her own signature spice for vegan meals with world-famous spice brand McCormick, was on the *New York Times* Best Seller list for both of her books, and won two NAACP

Image Awards. All of this seemingly from her kitchen, and at times, from others'. Although social media can be saturated and falsely curated, I believe in a huge portion of Tabitha's story, not because she's Southern and that in and of itself feels warm and relatable but because at most angles, no matter the position, Tabitha's space in the world via her kitchen table pushes against a narrative that on some level we have been made to believe. A narrative that states that a Black woman cannot be at once successful and intelligent, while also being able to literally feed you (and herself) in body and in spirit. From the screen, Tabitha is soft and strong. Open and private. Her work is extraordinarily nonpartisan. What she feeds us is what she has produced *for* herself. It carries and offers multitudes.

In a piece for Eater in June 2020—during the thick of the pandemic—as food insecurities within Black communities continued to crystallize, writer Jocelyn Jackson built a longstanding figurative table for women to sit shoulder to shoulder with other women across generations who have worked to sustain Black communities as a form of liberation. Georgia Gilmore, Ruth Beckford, and Fannie Lou Hamer were among those cited in Jackson's piece. The line that always comes to mind when reading Jackson's work is, "Food as Resistance."

For Georgia Gilmore, a midwife and cafeteria worker, the Montgomery bus boycott in 1956 was her lasting contribution to resistance. For 381 days, she fed protesters with the undercover group of women she organized, called the Club from Nowhere—and the money they raised helped fund the Montgomery Improvement Association (MIA). In addition to feeding folks like Martin Luther King, Jr., at her home, Georgia continued to feed protestors up until her death in 1990, the twenty-fifth anniversary of the Selma to Montgomery march.

Around the same time in the late 1960s when Georgia was in the throes of her work, the Black Panther Party developed the concept of "revolutionary intercommunalism," which consisted of building "survival programs" that would not only develop communities but sustain poor Black people in a positive way outside of the institutions that often forgot about them. Of course, this included a version of what we now know as our now federally run free-breakfast program, one of the largest forms of government welfare in the country. In Brooklyn alone, hundreds of thousands of public school families depend on daily free breakfast served before 8:00 A.M. to feed their children. The Black Panthers' Free Breakfast for Children program began in the safety net of St. Augustine's Church in Oakland, California. More than being a way to bolster morale, it served as a consistent source of meals, with frequently donated groceries like milk, grits, and eggs from whites and moderate Blacks. When asked by Eater about the Black Panthers' food program and the expansion of the government's free-breakfast program, former Black Panther member Norma Amour Mtume said this: "I really do believe that the government [expanded] their program because of the work we were doing."

In the 1990s, after Georgia's passing, and during the expansion of the breakfast program, I sometimes found myself inside a low-ceilinged dining room on the slanting top floor of a Bedford-Stuyvesant church. As a kid, I came to the church a few Sundays a year with my aunt, cousin, and uncle. After service—during which the choir sang twice, the collection plate was passed, and the sermon weaved back and forth between Bible times and our current time—we would take the narrow stairs up to the seven black and brown, round and rectangle tables to eat dinner. Barbecue chicken dangled off bones, and warm beets turned my fingertips pink. The church's table then, as it is now, was formative in the labor for Black liberation. After my cousin's grandpa (the church's pastor) passed, I watched as the honor was bestowed upon his daughter. She then sat at the center of the long table with her banana-yellow skin under her robes, as her sisters and parishioners fed her and other guests first. I knew to be in the kitchen and serve was a significant honor. I would peek in and watch in amazement as they moved about in that tiny dining room. The kitchen workers ate after everyone else did, but their roles were vital in the way of life, Blackness, and ministry: "'Bring the full tithe into the storehouse, so that there may be food in My house. Test Me in this,' says the LORD of Hosts. 'See if I will not open the windows of heaven and pour out for you blessing without measure.'" Like tithes, sustaining those so that we may sustain ourselves, what these folks got back for their efforts was tenfold.

In her Eater article, Jocelyn Jackson leans on the sustainable food system scholar Lindsey Lunsford to open and close her piece:

> As a Black woman in a racist and sexist world, I make two distinct choices on an ongoing basis: one is what I believe; the other is how I feel about those beliefs. As someone whose lineage after Africa reaches back to Mississippi and Kentucky, my family stories include the DNA of survival, and I choose to believe that my ancestors planned my presence for this very moment. Each time I get to feed my community, I feel the sacredness of this path I've chosen, one of social justice food projects bent on collective liberation.

Jackson reiterates a question that Lunsford poses: "How does food reveal the vulnerabilities and strengths of African Americans?" The conclusion seemed to be that soul food offers Black people the freedom to claim autonomy from, as she writes, "the white supremacist demonization of soul food" as unhealthy and inferior. "The 'first soul food,'" she adds, "was a Black woman's breast milk." I paused the first time I read this line in the article, looking down at my deflated chest. Mine, then, had already done much of its work. My milk fed each of my children for a combination of twenty-three months separately, exactly. Those days, I often considered how the choice to breastfeed in my early twenties irreversibly would shape the way my breasts may be utilized and sexualized. I dissented for me then and the two children who talk back to me now.

This protest is one of the longest you can imagine. In each generation, the movement has tended to the question of food—food as a form of mutual aid distributed to sustain activists, and food as the actual mode of protest.

In 2009, Michelle Obama was the first First Lady to plant a massive vegetable garden at the White House since Eleanor Roosevelt's victory garden during World War II. Working alongside schoolchildren, she planted her garden at the southwest end of the South Lawn. Many of the Obamas' meals consisted of the fruits and vegetables plucked from that garden. During her eight-year tenure as First Lady, she also managed President Obama's Let's Move! campaign, a task force established to tackle the "epidemic of childhood obesity." Most notably, Michelle Obama and the USDA introduced an overhaul of the food guide in 2011, called My Plate. The guide used primary-colored triangles on a plate to simplify healthier eating habits. The plate, which looked like a pie chart, did away with the complex visual of a food pyramid as a means to healthy eating. Instead of needing to calculate what was on the kitchen table, parents could simply look at it. Like the garden that Obama revamped before moving out of the White House in 2016 to seal its permanency, My Plate became Michelle Obama's lasting legacy. It was a visual serving tool that I couldn't unlearn. My plate, her plate, our plates, and our tables, by extension, often resembled the chart.

When asked how in the world I get my kids to eat healthy meals, I say, "Keep offering" and "There are really no other options in the house." Dinner is never, despite their insistence, just noodles. Veggies are chopped finely in pasta. Fruit is blended in their smoothies and sits beside their bowls at dinnertime. These days, basil-and-kale pesto takes up a portion of their plate. Bubbly sparkling water foams from their cups; our table is full. My approach to feeding our family is attached to the privilege of my own adult exposure—not only in my becoming a mother during the time Michelle Obama revamped how we looked at our plates but also in being in a relationship with a white man, who approached food differently because of his doctor father and stay-at-home mother. Although I was broke and relied on the women in my family for monetary help at times, I adopted and adapted some of this learned approach. I learned about composting, consumed only whole grain bread, refused the forgery of American cheese, and became upset at the mere thought of my most conspicuous pal, bologna.

The opportunity to question food and food systems isn't automatically granted to Black people, though we have spent generations turning it over and using food as a means of work and healing in spite of that.

My mother worked full-time. Unlike her mother, my mother cooked large meals only on Sundays, because that was the only day she could. Many mornings, she left for work before we left for school; at times, she returned late in the evening. Some dinners were delightfully

eaten as a family from light beechwood snack tables on the couch with a movie on the big screen. Some dinners were eaten in my mother's bed so she could at once put her feet up, watch TV, and eat under the comfort of her lavender blanket—a bottle of cold Pepsi fizzing on her nightstand.

Sometimes our dining table was full of my mother's creative projects. Often, she would stack her papers at one end, and we would eat at the other. Now, I do the same, and I perform small tasks with my children to draw the line in time between work and rest. "Let's clean it off!" I say. "River, you get the plates." Oak chimes in, "Where should I place your computer, Mama?" It didn't take long in the pandemic for me to see my dining room table clearly for what it had been all along: a meeting place of sorts. People circulated essays on this cosmic shift in the family home, but all I thought about was how in my houses the dining table has always been a multilingual object.

In an essay for Vox on the disappearance of the dining room table, Melinda Fakuade dives into the history of the dining room table, and the way its slow death preceded the pandemic.

> American culture also encourages workaholism, and that mindset bleeds over into our home spaces. Plus, vacation time, parental leave, and paid sick days are scarce in this country. No wonder we lost the dining room along the way. But all that doesn't mean people aren't interested in eating together. . . . Family life has changed significantly, and we don't necessarily learn about the world through dinner conversation anymore. It's all at our fingertips, and our interests when it comes to homemaking are much less heteronormative than before. The dining table, going back to even the ancient Greeks, is intertwined with societal power dynamics and gender roles.

The etymology of table is *mensa*—an altar, an object to workshop and to worship at. Words come easy at the dining table. I appreciate the writing scene in the dining room in the late afternoon, when the sun's low golden hue makes the painted blue walls look like tinted powder. The windows are open, and I type as I watch the plants in that room dance in the wind. Words come equally as easy in the morning at the kitchen table, sunshine streaming in and coffee in its place right next to my wrist. In our effort to analyze the accurate use of the dining room table, we erase the countless ways people and families not only make do but also thrive.

The table is not the facilitator; it is an object that aids in facilitating. On Sundays in my childhood homes, laughter reverberated off the walls, the kitchens were always blistering from on-all-day ovens, and my mother was never hungry at dinner because she'd been sampling chicken all day over the stove. We constantly talked over one another, as if our mouths couldn't ever catch up with our desire to say everything. I would lick my fingers, then quickly rinse them off at my mother's urging, only to return to the pot of rice and chicken I couldn't stay away from. We ate not at the table but on the bottom step of the stairs. The joy of being squished next to my cousins on a two-by-two step, bumping elbows and plastic forks; we shared thin paper plates with abandon.

Mommy, my grandmother, my mother, and other ancestors like Georgia Gilmore, the Black Panther Party—and even Michelle Obama—taught me that cooking is not a stagnant task. It is a living, breathing event—something that can make room, teach, speak, create. Ultimately, it's something that can resist. It is yours to choose. Food matters; people matter more. At the table, eating is secondary, but the life pulsing all around the table is primary—it's what compels everyone to gather there.

· · ·

"*Pushhhhh!*" I tell the kids as we shift the extendable table in the dining room, moving it off the wall. We are having vaccinated adult guests over for the first time in a long time. I am worried the kids won't know their way around the table. I am worried I won't know my way around other forms of life.

I made a veggie pasta, my signature dish when hosting. I've asked my friend N to bring food, too. I throw cheddar bunny crackers and popcorn in a bowl. Applesauce squeezers get placed on the table next to empty mason jars. N brings wine and extra treats for good measure. I light candles that are eager to show off their pastel colors and threaded wax. The light in the dining room dims to a hum. When the evening runs late, we dance—sweat starting to form on our brows and upper lips. We have snacked all evening, barely touching our plates. We dance like we're intoxicated, high on the hog, all euphoria and salty skin. The delusion is the normalcy of this moment in time.

The kids and I are used to solitary dancing. Every morning, I push the table back to its resting place while half asleep. My ceramic coffee mug replaces my wineglass. The boisterous evening music we'd played until our ears practically bled is swapped for soft and smooth Sam Cooke. I laugh at River, who has snuck into the room and crawled under the table to scare me while using her hands as crab claws at my ankles. Oak soon follows behind, mimicking her every move. The table is the boat. The floor is the sea. I am swimming with my children. Legs waving, arms wagging, we are tentacles and seaweed. Food is not my legacy. The table is not a construct of our love. We become as we always were—delighted singers, blowing raspberries on one another's stomachs until our bellies are full.

Homebody

Care is the antidote to violence.

—SAIDIYA HARTMAN

After a week away from Brooklyn during the spring of 2021, I am relieved to see the stretch of golden skyline as I cross the Brooklyn Bridge. I relax my curvy frame into the back of a taxi with the windows down, and the air smells of funk, subway—and life. The tiny storefronts overflow with people in masks vying for a slice of pizza, a cig, a cold drink, a warm place, or a simple conversation with someone unfamiliar. They squeeze side by side through narrow doorways, in storefront brownstones with their faces brushing cheek to cheek, and I giggle as I notice this each time.

The interaction reminds me of the way in which we enter our apartment, when multiple people are coming and going at once. Although the apartment is large, its entryway's three-way intersection is cumbersome. Between the cats, the kids, the babysitter, deliveries, and me, we squish under the wallpapered arch, and next to the built-in drawers, to navigate the interior. One exit leads to the dining room, which leads to the living room. The other, to the kitchen, which leads to the side yard. And the long stretch of hallway leads to the walk-in closets, bedrooms, and bathroom.

"You go first!" I say to my sitter. "No, you!" he asserts as we play our tap-in, tap-out game. His awareness of his body as a young, midsize Latino man, and mine, as a Black woman, in that space of the same age is something to watch, I'm sure. Eventually, we both grab the doorknob, knocking it off from its handle for the umpteenth time, only for me to screw it back on, claiming the maintenance people will come, and we both find our way out of that odd space.

I did not consciously consider this particular intersection when seeing this apartment for the first time back in 2017. I did love how each room felt like a surprise upon turning a corner. I didn't consider the architecture because, when I needed it, the apartment chose me. My ex-husband and I had just reluctantly re-signed a lease in a one-bedroom around the corner, where we split the bedroom into two with a temporary wall partition, with overhanging plants along the top for life. It was the ground floor of a brownstone and, between my land-lord's exorbitant ways and the exposure of our complexities and arguments that couldn't stay within our thin apartment walls, I got physically ill when I realized the ground was giving, and either way, I would be in that place or another place, mostly solo with two kids.

My finances and my body felt at risk at the sheer prospect. I had no real way to pay the increase in rent when my friend told me about her beloved space she was leaving. At the time, I was finishing my proposal for my first book, so there was hope. But hope often isn't enough. I lost twenty pounds that spring within two months. I sat on a disposable paper-covered doctor bed while my nurse at the clinic practically jiggled the loose skin from my bony arms and questioned if my predisposed depression was making its grand entrance and was the cause of the number on the scale.

"Are you sleeping?" she pressed.

"Not really," I quipped. "It's my youngest child . . ." I began to say. I grew silent. It wasn't.

"What have you eaten?" she continued.

"Everything is kind of foggy, and each day, the weight of the bed feels heavier. But I get up," I responded.

Was I silently having a resurgence of my childhood-diagnosed lupus? Was it the depression? She went on to explain what I needed to watch for, but also how my desire to sit on that medical bed in my colorful underwear one afternoon was a good sign. "Come back in a few weeks," she requested. I didn't. Two years ago, I logged on to that same health portal to check my blood type, and there it was: "*2017. Depression positive.*" After dropping my kids off at school, I walked four blocks on a rainy day to see my friend's newly available apartment in real life. She sat in a room speaking with her son and a house visitor, while her babysitter did a loose walking tour through dimly lit hallways. I try to remember what I ate that day I viewed the apartment—clementines by the handful come to mind, that is all.

I moved in three weeks after stepping foot in it, and I no longer starved in fear that stress would make me heave whatever was in my stomach back at my feet. I didn't snap at the sound of my landlord knocking at my door. Instead, I covered the living room in plants, the long white table in flora, and was dragged past my stoop by friends to jump a game of double Dutch at the playground to heal. I made love with someone new under the vaulted ceilings of a temple as the winter sun shined on my brown stretch-marked body, and I felt the gratitude in the sinner and the sanctified. I was holy ground; unfolded and vulnerable stratum.

We can't choose the bodies we inhabit, but for many of us, home is an intrinsically personal decision dreamed about for a lifetime and known within seconds of entering a place. Like sex, you know when two parts just fit. Architectural historian Beatriz Colomina opens her well-known argument in *Sexuality and Space* with this: "The politics of space are always sexual, even if space is central to the mechanisms of the erasure of sexuality." In that same body of work, Colomina looks at a house designed for Josephine Baker by Adolf Loos, one of the most influential European architects and theorists of the late nineteenth century. Loos repeated what he did in his other work, creating open spaces that looked like mirrors representing the Freudian psyche. The exterior wears a masculine mask; the spaces are ambiguous and split. "The eye is directed towards the interior, which turns its back on the outside world; but the subject and the object of the gaze have been reversed," writes Colomina. In the Baker house, which rids itself of domestic life entirely, there is a swimming pool that can be entered from the second floor. The pool, an often privatized activity, becomes the center as a salon. Colomina adds, "The most intimate space—the swimming pool, paradigm of sensual space—occupies the center of the house, and is also the focus of the visitor's gaze." She goes on, "But between this gaze and its object—the body—is a screen of glass and water, which renders the body inaccessible."

I had been obsessed with this architectural theory from Colomina since first reading it. I was stuck on her lines and, in truth, unable to read further because the first itch had been satisfied enough. But later, I read on and became even more of a devotee to the concept—and the social constructs and contradictions that spring from it. When explaining the misfortune of the Josephine Baker house, particularly Loos's philosophy behind it, Colomina summarizes:

> The image of Josephine Baker offers pleasure but also represents the threat of castration posed by the "other": the image of woman in water—liquid, elusive, unable to be controlled, pinned down. One way of dealing with this threat is fetishization.

> The Josephine Baker house represents a shift in the sexual status of the body. This shift involves determinations of race and class more than gender. The theater box of the domestic interiors places the occupant against the light. She appears as a silhouette, mysterious and desirable, but the backlighting also draws attention to her as a physical volume, a bodily presence within the house with its own interior. She controls the interior, yet she is trapped within it. In the Baker house, the body is produced as spectacle, the object of an erotic gaze, an erotic system of looks.

In the passages written by Colomina, she asserts that the visitors consume Baker's Black body as a surface adhering to the windows. Like the body, the house is all surface; it does not simply have an interior.

Folks consider the frame of their house and apartments—from build, to rental, to purchase. What we see first when entering matters: the height of the ceilings, the length of the hallway, how many windows make up each room, and if the house comprises an open layout. Before Colomina, there was urbanologist and sociologist William H. Whyte who spent years walking around New York City, observing how interactions with spaces affected people's socio-health. Whyte developed what architects and urban developers know today as *triangulation.* In triangulation, "strangers are more likely to talk to one another in the presence of such a stimulus. The stimulus might be musicians, or street entertainers, or a piece of outdoor sculpture."

I've lived in cities all my life, and I agree with Whyte's observations. When people go outdoors in the city, they don't blindly spread out. Their behavior suggests that it's comforting to engage with architecture, as well as the vibrant ways a place is intended to be used—gatherings in parks, working in buildings, shopping in stores, sitting on benches. Mental orientation is based on where our bodies are. Similarly, behavioral neuroscientist Kate Jeffery explains that no matter how beautiful a space is, when it comes to interiors, one must know how things relate to each other spatially. If not, we risk the negative effects of disorientation. For every singular person, the way a house fits their body and their family feels different, and this difference is often based on the relationship between the body and a given space. We are simply designed that way, whether it be a memory, a sexual experience, faulty gender norms, or instinct. But of course, there are robust limitations within those differences, too: money, time, how cold or hot the current rental market is, to name a few. For many, of course, the matter of *choice* about where we move our bodies simply does not exist at all. The architecture of the place that they call home has to work with and within the bounds of their living.

I am not sure when I came to know my body as this insubstantial piece of a larger puzzle. It could have started with my vitiligo—seeing the erasure of my Blackness dissolve into white patches, and my fight with and for my body to protect it as a result. Or it could have been the conversations I overheard from my bedroom when I was a kid, after I decided to write SEX on the bay window of my bedroom several times with a crayon. Or the time the top half of my wooden bunk bed fell on top of me as I lay in my sister's bottom bunk. All these things happened, but a dreamed-up version is what lives in my mind, rendering them as blueprints, the maps of some other life.

Perhaps it was the fall of 2018, bearing witness to the testimony of Christine Blasey Ford that fanned that ember of home and body obsession. I had just turned in my first book. I was proud. Tired. On an incredible, delusional high. The first proposal of that book included a home component, and thankfully, I did not succeed in adding it in, for what I know now about home is not what I knew then. The questions I had in 2018 only birthed more questions, and I became a ravenous brute. I found memories in drunken conversations in the backs of lounges or on my living room sofa, my friends slamming down the word *rape* like a stack of playing cards. Too many of them. And if they didn't use the word *rape*, they explained that it was a thing that went too far in their homes or in his. Or a time they said no, but their partner did it anyway. The stories piled up on top of Ford's. I became a well, as did my home, and I felt suddenly, collectively, terrified of what we all carried with us each day and the home in which I occupied.

What did happen? The alleged sexual assault by Brett Kavanaugh and Mark Judge became Ford's life secret living in between the walls of her home, like the stories from my friends lived in my own. The experience was bad enough to follow her around, but not bad enough to out him sooner, because in Ford's account, he did not rape her. "Over the years, I told very few friends that I had this traumatic experience. I told my husband before we were married that I had experienced a sexual assault. I had never told the details to anyone until May 2012, during a couples counseling session. The reason this came up in counseling is that my husband and I had completed an extensive remodel of our home, and I insisted on a second front door, an idea that he and others disagreed with and could not understand. In explaining why I wanted to have a second front door, I described the assault in detail," Christine shared with the Senate Judiciary Committee.

I began to lock my bedroom door every night in deep fear that someone was watching me enter and leave my home alone most days of the week. I contemplated the extra benefits and drawbacks of that three-way intersection in my apartment. I could see a perpetrator, and I could not. My kids weren't protected, and I was; I was awarded the benefit of consciousness (whether I liked it or not) that comes with listening, time, trauma, and age.

Before Ford, there was Anita Hill. She had preceded Ford testifying in front of Congress about the sexual harassment she had experienced as an aide to Clarence Thomas, who was a Supreme Court nominee in 1991. Anita Hill's story was discredited, despite mounting evidence around her statement.

There were also Sukari Hardnett and Angela Wright, both African American women who experienced Thomas's requests for dates, sexual propositions, and inappropriate conversations about porn and their own bodies. Although these women corroborated Hill's testimony, neither were called to take the stand, and Hill continued to be vilified by Republicans, Democrats, and the media. Thomas went on to become a judge on our highest court. Although I was just a baby, I recall hearing about Hill's story throughout my teen years. However, unlike Ford, whose own courageous statement was credited to Anita Hill's, Hill has remained staunchly private since the early '90s and her public testimony. We don't know how Clarence Thomas's transgressions affected her life at home.

Did she need a second door?

A master lock?

Are her ceilings low?

Is her bed high?

I know something happened to me, I said to my therapist one morning during a tear-filled session. "Something" has happened to one in four of us, according to the Department of Justice. It's hard to write that. It's impossible to say that. Even if not at its most heinous, any violation of one's body is a violation, ultimately, of one's home. "I was marked after that," Roxane Gay poignantly shares in *Hunger.* "Men could smell it on me, that I had lost my body, that they could avail themselves of my body, that I wouldn't say no because I knew my no did not matter. They smelled it on me and took advantage, every chance they got."

It was, is, has always been, something so other that I think I remember in dreams, or on days when I am discussing breasts and periods with my daughter, peppering our conversations with warnings and assurances: "You can come home if you want. I will always pick you up, no questions asked, if you need." And the earliest: "Your body is your body, and no one has a right to touch that body." "I know, Mommy," she asserts while we cuddle in bed each evening. Her brother overhears and yells back from his top bunk, "And my body is my body, too!"

I have made peace with a nonspecific faulty memory and how it folds and collects like dust in all of us like pool-house memorabilia.

July 4, 2014, I wore Oak on my chest in a white-and-blue wrap baby carrier in Coney Island as I did almost every day that summer when he was a newborn. I wove through a crowd with my ex and River walking ahead of me. I felt something—a bag, I thought—push up against my butt as I moved through the throng of people. I shifted my body to move out of the way. Farther we walked. I shifted again. I have grown accustomed to being aware of my body. Moving my body. Fighting for and with my body. Soon, as the something continued to move closer, pressing harder, I was struck by the realization that this wasn't a bag at all. I felt the tip of a penis on the deepest center seam of my shorts. I swung around with one hand on the head of my son, and the man disappeared into the crowd. We returned home, and at home, I dwelled on the thought that this was another thing that happened not only to my body but because my son was still so reliant on my body—on my breast, my arms, my back—it happened to his body, too.

We love the imperfections of a house, its creaky floorboards, the aged plaster, the old windows that still insulate as they ever did, and the moldings that show it existed before, during, and after the war. My body is not a victim. Nor is it a survivor. On the worst days, it is just my home with too many map pins of places and things that lead down to overgrown forests and slowly rebuilt rooms.

Gardens as rooms.

On good days, those rooms are wildflowers covering what lies still.

My body is a home, I say as I check the small U-locked door to the right of my bed once more. I lay a weighted quilt over my body, those maps. As of 1995, approximately 1.8 million adolescents ages twelve to seventeen in the United States have been sexually assaulted. Blacks and Natives are victimized much more than whites, most often by someone they know, and in their own homes. *Our bodies are homes*, we repeat. There are generations of people—their homes—both seamlessly becoming refugees, depositing into one another. Still, like magic, our bodies sprout flowering black-eyed Susans and butterflies, cicadas and sweet peas, in front of our untended and fertile buildings—spaces folks don't think to help restore.

One evening as summer waned and the prospect of moving again stuck to my skin like glue, I read and soaked my achy joints with lavender Epsom salt. It felt like hours in that oversize tub of mine. Oftentimes, as my body wears down, I can only truly feel its worth when I exercise it or soak it. I soaked that evening until I got wrinkly. I soaked until my toes got soggy and my fingers looked like coral reefs. I adorned my body in my favorite robe that was hung on the door— the same door I lock every night—plaid, chocolate, and taupe fabric draped over my almond-oiled skin. I get dressed at night after these soaks, as I do during the day, as I did as a child, in my Sunday best—regardless of the day of the week.

After-dark programming was my real first teacher in sex education. Taxicabs became therapists' offices, and cameras followed ordinary couples home to hear about their sexcapades in *Real Sex*. I was a child of the '90s with a twenty-inch TV and about five channels available. Somehow, HBO was available on one of the five any time after ten o'clock, which was great for me because I was already an insomniac at twelve years old. I grabbed the little black remote, crawled close to the edge of my bed, and watched shows kids shouldn't watch in my kid room full of stuffed Winnie the Poohs and purple boxes full of sparkly nail polish and hair clips. Anne and Bob, in their living room, chatting about their occasional threesomes. Steve and Tim talking about being gay and what went where. The tongues and the thrusting, all available to me. I wasn't interested in sex, per se. I was interested in the comfort, exploration, and normalization of people's bodies within their homes when they assumed no one else was watching. None of the people I saw on those shows were Black or Native or even Latino. And maybe more than sex, the lesson in who gets to do what and where, from my childhood room with pink blankets, moving-eye dolls, and B2K posters, became even clearer.

Two months before Donald Trump became president of the United States, confirming and reaffirming the struggles and the hate for not only Black life but for immigrants of any origin that shape this nation, I sat in a third-row seat at Brooklyn Academy of Music and sobbed while watching *Moonlight*. Filmmaker Barry Jenkins tells the story of Chiron, a.k.a. Little, as he grows up, Black, and traverses an unconscious exploration of masculinity and sexuality. Each story and scene is as complex as it is in real Black life. For every moment, there is meaning. Like the near baptism that Little experiences as he learns to swim in the ocean with Juan, mentor and father figure, who admittedly also sells drugs to Little's mother. Water, as a body and within the body, and on the body, washes over us and these two Black moonlit men. In the film and in life, water is the guide and a wild monster with incredible ability to nurture and heal. Not only is Little's head cradled by Juan in the depths of the ocean, but it is also there as Little boils water on his gas stove, fills the tub with the warmed water and dish soap, and pours it over his head in his off-white-and-yellow-tiled bathroom to cleanse himself.

Maybe this is why Black mothers birthing in tubs and in birthing pools have always stopped me in my tracks. The thought of not having a baby ever again is at times stalled by the memory of that strange intoxicating high I got after birthing Oak without medication in the hospital after a thirty-six-hour labor. Before Oak, there was another room and a D&E under sharp light, where I hope I dreamed about the water carrying me over the threshold from pregnant to mourner, from pain to healing. And before the D&E, and the Pitocin that dripped within me, I laid my twenty-one-year-old body in the tiny tub of our slanted railroad apartment in Bushwick, following waves of intense contractions with my legs hung over that tub, my fingers ripping at the cast, until I gave in to the help that not only my baby but my body needed to transition to the other side.

"*Ring of fire!*" women howl through panting breaths. The statement is a sort of safe word for explaining the process of a baby's head moving through the birth canal and vagina. The tissues in the vagina stretch to make room for the baby's soft skull. Traditionally, this defining transition is called *crowning*. Some women don't feel the intensity of the stretching, and for others like myself, the stinging and the winding is an easy recollection on any given day. With River, I didn't feel the ring. I only felt the several-inch tear after my epidural wore off and the skin of my vagina was snipped through. I still have a scar. With Oak, he stayed put in his first home in my body to the very last possible day, despite being the child I worried would exit my body well before he was able to live outside of it. During that labor, I felt myself open, and I allowed the fire to take over not only my vagina but my entire being. I consented to my body moving in the way it needed to release this baby that desired to be. A gush of water and blood pooled in my brown palms as I went to guide him out of my body, our once shared space.

In a piece for *The Atlantic*, Leah Wright Rigueur explores the beauty, complexity, and ultimately, the free joy Black mothers desire. Rigueur spoke to teachers, historians, academics, and stay-at-home mothers, asking each of them: "What does free Black motherhood look like to you?" Many of the women had no answer. But the ones who did stood out.

Theresa Thames, the associate dean of religious life and the chapel at Princeton University, shared, "Freedom for Black mothers looks like walking through the world living and thriving, without bracing yourself for the trauma that results from white supremacy."

Rigueur closed the essay with a distinct vision of a Black mother pealing into laughter, an intimate witness of Black women free from the constant association to pain in their body, the only way they eventually access joy.

In 2021, the American Academy of Pediatrics reported that over 2 percent of births at home happened to non-Hispanic white women. In a *Mother Jones* piece that looked at births in low-income communities, they noted that these statistics often overlook the many Black women who spent time in their showers and tubs ushering new life into the world during that same year, not just because of the coronavirus. Those same statistics show that Black women are three times more likely to die in maternal care, and the desire to birth at home was because they'd like to access a world where living and thriving came without bracing for the impact of trauma, which Thames spoke of.

The people who have cared for my children, whether women or men, have always been maternal figures. As Oak has gotten older, I've started to remember something I had repeated aloud during my birth with him. The words felt so visceral: "No one is helping me!" I wailed. I would go in and out, moving through his birth while sitting and standing. "No one cares. No one helps me!" I continued, until a tiny nurse came and wrapped a blanket around my hips to shake him out. I did not use medication, and in truth, I have been obsessed with that nurse as a physical embodiment of my own strength wrapped into hers.

I suppose what I'm attempting to define in my strange back-of-the-throat longing to move through the birth process once again is also a deep desire to reconnect to myself and readdress various phases and places this body inhabits. Black women and women of color are constantly at risk with their bodies— a narrative we've heard over and over again, exhaustingly, seeping into every generation. Every day, we work to shift this paradigm. We desire freedom for the sake of freedom. However, at the same time, each and every day we choose to lay our achy joints in the water, in that corner bathroom, in that old tub, to meet our bodies, as we undo the taut tie of freedom and risk. Collectively, we wade in that water as both reprieve and protection.

It has been four years since the kids and I moved into this apartment in 2017. I dream of something beyond it. And equally, I am distressed about the logistics of it. "I'm stressed about the apartment," I text my mom in the spring after the realtors, their builders, and the buyers had left the apartment we were asked to move out of. "Wait. Pray. It will come," she calmly and confidently responds. But I am not good at waiting, and I'm unsure if God hears my ridiculous prayers in a season of so much worldly despair.

Summer is crawling into autumn now, and to my heart's reluctance, when I am out at night and get a glimpse of the city and its skyline, I tend to think of whatever future apartment we will inhabit. Does it have ten windows? Is it a brownstone? A two-bedroom? What is the shape of the bathroom, and will I know upon entrance if it is the best kind of tub for soaking this brown, complex, and joyful body? When I sit at my desk and peel myself away from searching for apartments, I tend to think of the many men, women, and children who have decided to stake claim to wherever they need to call home. In her book *Upheavals of Thought*, philosopher Martha Nussbaum writes, "We cannot understand [a person's] love . . . without knowing a great deal about the history of patterns of attachment that extend back into [the person's] childhood. Past loves shadow present attachments, and take up residence within them."

When my children were younger, I thought about the teachers I observed walking down city streets, beautifully directing fourteen or eighteen toddlers along a sidewalk, blowing music from their lips. While crossing a busy street, they would point to a stoplight, and even engage a car—"Say hi to the car!" the teacher would shout. The car always honked back. They sang songs that we adopted, too, as we crossed the street: "We're waaaallllkinnggg! We're waaaallllkinnggg!"

As kids, River and Oak noticed everything about the way a building looked from the outside, a sconce, a mailbox, a railing, overgrown window boxes. I don't believe we suddenly grow up and stop needing and noticing the multitudes of the architecture we live among every day. Minds and souls live as touch points and entry points that also remind us of one true fact: no matter what spaces we occupy, our bodies are our longest and most intimate homes.

LE

How the Magnolia Grew

the earth is a living thing
is a favorite child
of the universe

—LUCILLE CLIFTON

"There are men climbing up on the tree!" the kids shouted from their bedroom window that overlooks the cement backyard. It was barely 9:00 A.M., and I was having one of those easy mornings that mothers dream of, especially single mothers in a pandemic. I looked through the window, and there the men were: vinyl ropes strung around our tree's oversize arms, ladders suddenly strewn all over the place, our furniture pushed about like mismatched puzzle pieces. It was a sunny late-spring morning, and I just decided to stop watching Governor Cuomo's and Mayor de Blasio's daily press briefings while folding clothes on the couch. It was best to wean off, as the number of deaths slowly ticked down from one thousand a day. *A relief,* I thought that morning. *Only four hundred.*

Our tree was an *Ailanthus altissima,* the tree of heaven. It was healthy, roughly fifty years old, and cooled the backyard during the near one-hundred-degree summer days. Although it is known on the New York arbor beat as an invasive species, I welcomed its long-lived presence as a sign of perseverance, à la *A Tree Grows in Brooklyn.* "Who wants to die? Everything struggles to live," writes the author, Betty Smith.

The neighbors in the yard behind mine, a French family who had purchased their $3 million carriage house earlier that year, had waged a quiet war with my ever-desperate-for-money landlord. The tree, they asserted, could drop a branch out of nowhere and kill one of their children. It wasn't just a fast thought, they shouted from the other side of their fence, while the men swung back and forth, attempting to ready the tree limbs to be snapped one by one. I later realized the neighbors had artificial grass where grass would typically grow, which told me all I needed to know. Despite their assertions, I don't think they were truly convinced the tree would harm their children. I believe they did what select newcomers often do when given enough land, time, and immense wealth: they claim *more.* The tree wasn't on their yard, but they knew that, when threatened with a lawsuit and the lift of the removal cost, my landlord would accept their offer. It was worth it to them to deprive my children, River and Oak, with their earthbound names.

The kids and I ran outside in our pajamas, morning eyes and breath. They sobbed about the tree while I patted their backs and yelled at the men, simultaneously calling my landlord as any sane tenant and mother would. I called other tenants and neighbors, too, to stage a sit-in until we sorted it out. "So many people are dying right now! Why would you choose to kill a living thing at this very moment?" After two hours of a standoff, where I refused to move and the workers refused to cut, the arborist arrived and said the tree was healthy, though it could use some trimming. Eventually, the workers collected their things, pieced my yard furniture back together incorrectly, and agreed that there was too much tension around the death of the tree to proceed. I had tried to find a middle ground: "What if you plant a new one in its place? What about trimming it back?" The neighbors seemed inclined to pet me, but I knew they wouldn't give up the course. My kids rested in the fact that the fight was done for today, and in the end, the land we rented was not ours to truly control for the long run either. "One day, we'll have our own, and we'll make our own decisions, and we will plant a bunch of trees!" I said to soothe their aching hearts and mine.

My mother was everyone's go-to for flora information, but we didn't have many living plants in our house. They were too much to manage under the strain of single parenting and full-time work. Instead, my childhood home had one nearly seven-foot silk (fake) palm of which my mother was incredibly proud and which became an omen of goodwill. We also had a (real) Boston fern that rotated through rooms like a changing guard. As children, we dusted off the leaves of the big palm when they began to turn gray with dust and lifted the shreds of black-and-brown faux soil so that it looked as if authentic earth was tucked around our plant.

Each time we had to make a new house a home, her beloved plant (along with a large quintessential '90s Black jazz print, with Black dancing figures in blue and purple garments) was the first thing that she placed to make it feel like our space. What my mother lacked in other things of the earth, she made up for in several children. We replicated the same cycle of life.

"Look at what she's digging up!" I remember my grandmother's best friend excitedly shouting at me when they took me to a community garden during an afternoon walk when I was no more than nine. She was my mother's god-mother, and after she passed away from breast cancer, I remember noticing a change in our capacity to hold not just many truths but many people. We could see all of those who came before us as still being with us in everything we touch, only refined. It was true for my grandmother, too. When I walked with her from one grassy plot to the next, she spoke of her best friend fondly, recall-ing the ways the earth mattered to them both. Her love of earth was evident in the tinctures she mixed in the kitchen with things purchased at her beloved health food store, things from the soil that she believed aided blood cells and biome: elderberry, goldenseal, echinacea, rose hip, and chamomile.

When we visited my father, he had two plants, too, although I can't recall which kinds they were. One was next to his bed, the soil of which I reverently inspected as my eyes darted to his seemingly always-bare feet, as he sat on his bed talking to my siblings. He briefly bent over to speak with me, not about the plant but about the soil, as if to compare it to the soul of the organism and how well was its steward. What he said then was similar to something he shared with me about a person's feet and caretaking a few years prior: "All you have to do is look at a person's feet to see how well they care for themselves. That's one of the ways I fell in love with your mom." I remember things mostly in relation to how they live and how they died. And in some cases, how they didn't live at all.

·   ·   ·

In my home today, my apartment in Brooklyn, there are no silk plants. Instead, nearly a dozen real plants call my apartment home, propped in corners like furniture. They are positioned with design in mind, such that a visitor could nearly forget their true function. But I cannot, because the plants require a level of attention and weekly, sometimes daily, care that asks me to bind my being to theirs.

If you look carefully, even at an indoor plant, you can watch their comings and goings; if you're vigilant, you'd be good to listen, too.

Oak is just as fascinated by the enormous fiddle in our living room as I was with my father's plants and my mother's silk palm. He asks for a mason jar to perform a one-man relay from the sink to the living room in order to water it. When the air in our apartment has been suspicious, I've used the history of plants as a cleansing property. "This will help us," I tell my children as I choose a new plant from our local garden store. "Another one?" they raise as I carry it on our walk home, mentally mapping where its place will be.

Despite their complaints, my children have learned the act of propagation as much as I know which plant prefers which corner at a specific time of year. As soon as a plant has established itself in our order, they take the shears, cut a piece of its roots, grab a recycled jelly jar, fill it halfway with water, and place it on their windowsill, under the sun, to watch it grow. I have tried to have plants accompany them in their bedroom, but Oak's sleep has been inconsistent since he had his open-heart surgery. Sometimes he has detailed dreams he animatedly shares with me in the morning. Other times he calls them nightmares, rattling and tangible, tears streaming down his face in the wee hours of the morning as I hang over his bunk. I am nearly certain he is seeing someone, people now gone— a belief cemented when speaking with spiritual friends who urge I find a way to ease the discomfort of that opened portal. A strange tie between two worlds that most people, let alone children, are not accustomed to, only made accessible to him by the three hours his heart remained on a heart-lung bypass machine. In the darkness when he awakes and is unaware what to do with what he's found on the other side, plants become figures that exacerbate his dreams, so we've done without them in their room, to care for his heart in this realm, in this way. In lieu of plants, there is an oversize mural on one of their walls, painted by my friend and artist Jenna Gribbon. The mural shows a hearty oak tree, an oversize trunk and the brown bush nearly swaying on a sunny blue day. There's grass around the tree, but more prominent is the wide river, wrapping its body around the oak to protect it.

"We care and we keep in this house," I tell the kids whenever a fight ensues. I do not need to point to the mural or the plants.

Oak requests to water the fiddle in the living room. He has since I first received it as a gift from my upstairs neighbor. To water it, he must be willing to do the labor of removing the hammer-smashed terra-cotta I layered over the soil to prevent our cat, Langston, from claiming it as his toilet. It was a trick I learned after months of trying and realizing that the cat's paws find the soil comforting and natural. Langston is unable to deny the call of home in some regard back to his own ancestral history, despite his domesticity. Oak removes the terra-cotta shards slowly to avoid cutting himself, placing them in a pile on the wood floor. He counts how many times he fills the jar with water before the soil is moist and the excess flows from the bottom. Despite his exposure to many plants in many rooms, he remains fascinated by the enormity of our hearty fiddle. Known scientifically as *Ficus lyrata*, it is one of the more difficult plants to keep alive and see thrive. "Nature has wired us to feel protective of babies, with their oversized, floppy heads. The big, round leaves of a fiddle leaf fig tree make it the houseplant equivalent of a newborn," wrote Michelle Slatalla in a *Gardenista* article, declaring the fiddle the "it" plant of the moment. In my apartment, it isn't just style that makes me love it, the way the fiddle leaf abuts my lavender modular sofa; it is the act of keeping it well. It is an everyday reminder that despite its finicky nature, together we have kept it viable, alive, and thriving—a projection of what I, too, hope to be.

Before the fiddle, the first projection I had of this sense of viability was in the form of Hattie Carthan's painted portrait on the side of a building in Bedford-Stuyvesant. I stared at it reverently as a kid every time I passed it on the street. Portraits of Black ancestors were tangible idols for community and activism for Black kids like myself. They punctuated bricks, bodegas, and even churches, from Dumbo to Brownsville. These portraits were often created by rogue artists telling a story just by the smile, or hair, or maybe the item the sitter was holding in their hands. Carthan's portrait situated her near a garden—that placement alone told me she did something meaningful with her hands and the land. In the 1960s, before the Bronx began to burn and Bedford-Stuyvesant faced disinvestment, Carthan saw the direct correlation between earth matter and Black matter. In her sixties at the time, she began a grassroots effort that was known as one of the earliest radical approaches to funding and reinvestment known to New York City, according to the New York Preservation Archive:

> In 1966, she invited newly-elected Mayor John Lindsay to the block association's annual barbecue fundraiser, earning from the mayor an unlikely but powerful endorsement that drew city-wide attention to the block association's cause and provided a platform for her visibility and influence in the community to rapidly grow. By the end of the decade, Carthan was presiding over one hundred block associations in Bed-Stuy, which she chaired under the umbrella Bedford-Stuyvesant Beautification Committee, and advising the New York City Parks Department on numerous city-wide tree planting programs. Under her leadership, the beautification committee planted more than 1,500 ginkgo, sycamore, and honey locust trees throughout Bed-Stuy.

It wasn't just the committee. Known playfully as "the Tree Lady of Brooklyn," Hattie Carthan led a campaign to preserve a historic *Magnolia grandiflora* tree in front of her home at 679 Lafayette Avenue in Bed-Stuy. The magnolia was planted in 1855 by William Lemken and was able to thrive in Brooklyn despite its native desire to be in a warmer climate. After successfully winning her fight to protect the statuesque magnolia tree, Carthan fundraised to match dollars donated by the Horticultural Society of New York to build a protective wall for the tree. As of 2021, the *Magnolia grandiflora* is the only individual living landmark in New York City.

Although Carthan passed away in 1984 at eighty-three, her work would have overlapped with the community work of my young grandmother. She spent her days as a substitute teacher under the brash mayoral reign of Ed Koch. Among other fatal incidences that caused anger and outrage during Koch's tenure, four unarmed Black teens were shot in an act of racially motivated violence by a white man, Bernhard Goetz, for asking for five dollars, which Goetz described as an attempted mugging. All four boys were injured, and one became a paraplegic with brain damage, after being shot one more time by Goetz while he stated, "You don't look too bad. Here's another." Goetz was acquitted of all but one charge (third-degree criminal possession of a weapon) and went on to be a celebrity of sorts, hailed by famous New Yorkers like Joan Rivers for "arming himself."

Five years later, in '89, the year I was born at Downstate Medical Center in Brooklyn, my grandmother was on the sidewalk of Eastern Parkway in Prospect Heights with her girlfriends, just a few blocks from the community garden and across from the Brooklyn Botanic Garden, cheering for the first Black mayor of New York City, David Dinkins. Unrest, racial violence, and frustration continued to unfold and remained at the forefront of Dinkins's short mayoral tenure. Nevertheless, people like my grandmother unconsciously or consciously carried on the spirit of Carthan by staying close to their communities and digging in to weather the storms. They chose to replant and grow, not only in the reedy spaces allotted to them but wherever they saw a plot, a tree, a bed, a church, or a person to sow into.

In a 2021 illustration, my friend, the artist Mona Chalabi, depicted the probability of anti-depressant prescriptions in relation to tree density and population. With tonal shades of green (used to represent land and trees) and pops of yellow (to represent anti-depressant medication), Chalabi illustrated the higher likelihood of mental health issues in areas lacking green space. These areas of low tree density more often appear in poorer neighborhoods. She based her visuals on research by environmental psychologists Melissa Marselle, Diane Bowler, Jan Watzema, David Eichenberg, Toralf Kirsten, and Aletta Bonn, who were fascinated by the correlation between green spaces and socioeconomic status. I felt this palpable contrast whenever I shepherded the kids under the eastern white pine in Fort Greene Park, in March through early June during the height of the pandemic. When I did not know what would happen next, and fear would slither up from my pinkie toe to my esophagus, we sat under the tree's canopy and watched the season change day by day. We depended on that space for comfort and consistency. It kept us healthy and alive.

When the peak of the coronavirus subsided—the freezer trucks full of those we lost driven to the final resting places where they rightfully belonged—River, Oak, and I picked vegetables in a small tucked-in plot in our backyard, which overlooked one of the most overwhelmed public hospitals in Brooklyn. What was living and what had died became a preoccupation of mine. On our stoop, we planted beds of sweet peas and daffodils. In our backyard, sage, dill, and basil were buried shoulder to shoulder. We plucked. God plucked. And we harvested.

One day during this time, I sat atop a large rock on a hill twenty feet away from Oak and watched him in reverence. From afar, I saw him carefully remove a radish from the packed earth. He dug with his uneven nails, wiggling it out inch by inch, until he grabbed hold of it with the fullness of his hand and held it above his head. He swung it above his skullcap-covered curls, showing me his vegetable like some mighty prize. I can't forget the smile on his face, full of wonder and enchantment of what he beheld, in juxtaposition with the wrought-iron gate and building behind him—a simple physical partition—separating life from death.

Throughout my years of deep mourning—my father, my grandmother, an unborn child of mine, and all the people I've known and lost, including versions of myself—I've realized plants have been there as a well of transitory comfort. I am not judged in their presence, not even when I am snot-nose crying on the couch contemplating my own fragility in the evolution of the world. When I've needed to, I've talked to them while watering them. I've felt the *Sansevieria trifasciata*, the *Philodendron* and the *Chamaedorea seifrizii*, the *Pachira aquatica* hold me in a way flesh could not bear. When I was twelve, I was mesmerized with a single Bible verse, returning to it again and again: "By the sweat of your face you shall eat bread, till you return to the ground, for out of it you were taken; for you are dust and to dust you shall return." Early on, we are conditioned to believe death is a curse, from which our earthly selves will be raised as a return to glory. I have, for better or worse, found that plants exemplify this complexity, challenging our choice, and our will, to live.

In 2020, the summer before the tree was cut, Black Lives Matter protests erupted in front of my door in Brooklyn. I watched protests on my stoop with my children folded under my arms, unable to stop the tears from rolling out of my eyes. I was far too weary to march again. I was tormented by the palpability of feeling unwelcome and culled like cattle into danger and violence whenever a white supremacist or even a "well-meaning" white person felt like it. That summer, I read a piece by Robin Wall Kimmerer titled "On Choosing to Belong to a Place." In it, she poses, "Here is the question we must at last confront: Is land merely a source of belongings, or is it the source of our most profound sense of belonging? We can choose."

I chose a sense of belonging nearly a year later, when the chance arose in the form of a turn-key three-bedroom, three-bath home a few feet from the Hudson River. I jumped through every frenzied hoop to prove my own worth, while imagining a space for my children to learn and to share. Twice, I delivered three months of profit and loss statements, six months of savings, and declared many times that it was just me buying the house. History says the land was owed to me. But how could I own what was owed to us all? I couldn't shake the residual ache of the tree being cut down in contrast with the inexhaustible number of lives lost that season. Had all people felt this tired and tied to the land? Had they struggled with the climactic, often-white proprietorship, and wondered about their place in the matter? There were articles and podcast episodes by the dozens about Black farmers, their history, and ultimately the debt we owe them. Biden had just won the presidential race, and news of generations of harm on the farmers as a course to correct was in every news cycle. If any one group could help me ease the unsettling nature, they could.

I closed on the Mae House in late May. A month later, in June, our tree in Brooklyn was finally chopped down in the wee hours of the morning while the kids picked blue irises and drew floor plans for a two-story treehouse, which they hoped we'd have upstate. Like I had with death, I became obsessed with the track to become an *owner*. Somewhere in my lineage, I felt instinctively, the land belonged to me and I belonged to it.

"It looks like many years ago, someone had planted things, and now the wild is mixing with what was planted here intentionally." Magdonna pointed and explained as she walked the property—along the edge of the yard, in front of the

Mae House garage, standing next to the driveway, beside the bed of daylilies that were just beginning to bloom.

"Hmm, what's that?" I said, gesturing to a sheaf of deep green leaves on the black swing gate.

"That's clematis. Clematis climbs and is really beautiful, but you want to have it training up then going down on all of those things. What you could do is get a cedar arch with cedar limbs, and the clematis will be really happy as it makes its way around the arbor." She quickly moved her body down the hill of the yard as her child ran about the other side.

"Oh, this is an elm tree. Elms are endangered in our area, so you should keep it, but possibly replant it farther away from the house. They'll get huge. It's truly amazing how the elm does so good on this side of the river. On the other side, they don't appear and certainly don't thrive," she continued as she tugged at leaves, bent at nearly eye level to most. "This is goldenrod; it's a medicinal plant. It heals wounds, and is wonderful to be buried with."

Goldenrod, to heal minor wounds, to conceive into tea. To go home, with, everlastingly.

The Mae House sits on the land that belongs to the Mohicans, but I once read that it was the Cherokee who drank the goldenrod to cure all kinds of respiratory illnesses. Goldenrod, *Solidago*, "to make whole." By the time I made it down the hill to join her, Magdonna was already nibbling at ground ivy and echinacea. "Here, taste it," she urged as she split it into two, simultaneously teaching me how to separate and how to share with neighbors each season. "The plants are happier that way, you know!" she noted as our feet guided us to something new.

When my friend Alexa recommended Magdonna as a way to appraise the Mae House land, I was eager and nervous. My mind is too full of information most of the time, and although I have an indoor-plant green thumb, what existed outside, what existed naturally, always unnerved me. Of course, Black folks have been working the land for years—generations. Maybe it was the enormity of the task that kept me off-kilter, made me hesitant about rolling up my sleeves and putting my own hands in the soil.

It was a sultry August morning when I turned on NPR with my coffee at the dining room table and listened to an episode that focused on a Black family–owned farm in Windsor, New York. On the landing page of the episode, a thin Black man wears an oversize black T-shirt that reads BLACK LIVES MATTER in white block letters. Atop his head is a netted black trucker hat with a white face and black words that read MAKE FARMERS BLACK AGAIN. On his left is a thin Black woman with short blond hair and a gray paisley long-sleeved shirt. They look familiar, but I do not know them. The background of the photo is lush, overgrown green. James Minton, the owner of the farm, is eighty-five; he and his wife, Wilhelmina, have been married for over sixty years. After spending forty years in a Harlem apartment, they chose to relocate to a twenty-acre farm with a pond full of fish, a barn with one cow, three hundred egg-laying chickens, and maple trees from which Minton collects sap for syrup each winter. In the photographs, there are several young Black girls with braids and colorful beads running through the fields with younger children on their hips. There are towering teenage boys who create an assembly line that allows a package to travel from one hand to the next, until it reaches its final spot on the farm. When Minton retired a decade ago, he purchased the farm and left his apartment with Wilhelmina. The generations of children in the photos are Minton's grandchildren and great-grandchildren. The segment explained that the farm would be financially prosperous once the Mintons can manage to sell one thousand dozen eggs each week. But James and his grandson Daryl said success also means building a place where the family's youngest members can learn to care for the animals and the land.

James used his retirement money to purchase the land and many of the things to work off of it, which cost upward of $50,000. As of the time the NPR piece aired, they were still paying down the mortgage; he lamented that the struggle for Black folks to buy and live off what they owe is a stain on the government that we pay to help sustain us. The scene in my backyard, and my own journey for finding and owning land, suddenly hits me like a ton of bricks. Although I could never become a keeper of a farm, I had solidified plans for six garden beds with wormlike irrigation systems that I hoped would sprout herbs on the shady side of the garden and vegetables on the sunnier side.

On June 23, 2021, three days before my children ended their public school year and twenty-four days since I closed on the house, news broke that a judge blocked the $4 billion relief program set to be distributed to Black farmers and farmers of color. The judge cited its strict application to only farmers of specific racial backgrounds "irrespective of any other factors." However, the relief (which was part of a $4 billion Covid bill) was a restoration of decades of redlining, racism, and discrimination, openly admitted by the USDA. "Black people remain underrepresented in agriculture. Black Americans own just 1% of rural land nationwide. While 13.4% of the country's population is Black or African American, Black farmers make up 1.34% of all farm producers. In New York, where there are nearly 58,000 farmers, the 2017 U.S. Department of Agriculture (USDA) Census counted only 139 Black farmers in the entire state," says Jillian Forstadt. The small lot of Black farmers still wring their hands for their payments as the case is argued.

I wonder if any great trees fall during the interminable waiting.

"To name the world as gift is to feel one's membership in the web of reciprocity." I read these words by Robin Wall Kimmerer on the evening of my final harvest at the Mae House during our first year there. I had taken the train back to the city with a bouquet of yellow marigolds, curly kale, purple coneflower, and cosmos in my woven bag. I tucked sweet tomatoes in my pocket and nearly attempted to pluck the yarrow and aster the kids and I planted earlier that spring to protect the raised beds from the bunnies and the field mice that call the land home. When I got back to the city, I split my bundle into thirds, sharing part with my neighbor next door who had watched the kids for me a few weeks back, another with my friend who had encouraged me during a season of grief, and some in my own fridge for the kids and me. Over the summer, the kale, spinach, basil, and thyme had dwindled because of guests we hosted at the house whom we urged to use what we grew. TAKE WHAT YOU NEED, LEAVE THE REST! was written in chalk on a sign in front of the chicken-wire fence that protected the six beds.

If our first response is gratitude, then our second is reciprocity: to give a gift in return. What could I give these plants in return for their generosity?

"If you're going to do raised vegetable beds, I would put them right here!" Magdonna said the summer prior when I closed on the house. "It's perfect because this spot is in part sun and part shade, so you can diversify what you plant." When it was time for Katherine the carpenter to build the raised garden beds, we chose hemlock over oak and placed them where Magdonna directed. Before building, I found an old photo of the yard; an oversize toolshed stood where the beds were to be. I heard from my realtor that it likely burned to the ground many years prior to my ownership and even prior to the owners before me.

I had been nervous about this endeavor to grow my own garden upstate, even so far as having native flowers hand-painted on the walls of the primary bathroom before we planted that spring, in the event nothing grew. "At least we'll have some native plants," I joked with my friend Nina, who painstakingly worked her magic over two days, dipping her round brush in Parma gray paint.

Over time, my nerves dissipated when I considered the work of greats like art activist Linda Goode Bryant, who in 2009 started Project EATS, a nonprofit spurred by a documentary she watched of people in Haiti eating mud pies—a special kind of mud (believed by locals to be high in nutrients) mixed with margarine and salt, eaten to stave off the pangs of hunger—and realizing that the circum-stances (high prices and inaccessible food) weren't so different in cities like hers. Her work with Project EATS spans over five farms that use living installations that help directly feed the communities where they're based: Brownsville, the Belmont section of the Bronx, and East Harlem, to name a few. Community members can actively engage in the art and in the food, under Bryant's powerful mantra, "Use what we have to create what we need." Bryant's work also as a sin-gle mother and artist who founded Just Above Midtown (or JAM) in 1974 in New York City (with several locations after evictions), for diverse artists who were left out of mainstream institutions and galleries at the time, was equally inspir-ing. She not only made room for her children in the spaces she created but of and for artists who were parents themselves. Artists like the incomparable David Hammons, who, in the summer of 2020, when River, Oak, and I visited Hudson and stayed in a smoke- and dog-scented rental, came to us as we stood under his African American flag flown at half-staff a few feet away from the Amtrak station, overlooking the Hudson River. It was hung under the direction of Kamal Johnson, the first Black mayor of the city. While we looked at the train tracks and basked in our first "Covid vacation," David pointed out tiny rips in the flag that needed to be gently repaired. He spoke of Hudson's past as an old whaling town and of the Black people who first found a home in Hudson. He spoke of gentrification, of being pushed out, of 9/11, and of making art in hard times, by us and for us. He snapped a photograph of our mask-clad faces under his flag, and asked Oak, "Do you know who I am?"

I reminded O of an early photograph of David—he was the man with the snowballs, who many years ago invited folks to play, touch, and experience art and resistance. It wasn't just Linda and David who did this kind of work—they had paved the way for others in the tiny city of Hudson as well. It was also Nkoula Badila of Grow Black Hudson, too. Her movement to reintroduce

Hudson's Black and brown community to the importance of healing through growing one's own food began that same summer of 2020 as a way to guide folks on what they *could* do and always *knew* to do. Nkoula's work was small in size and large in impact. Gardens graced Hudson stoops; raised beds donned four-foot-by-four-foot plots behind bent iron gates. Through the bounty and through the community, Nkoula teaches people about this spiritual/land connection through a series of acts funded by others through one another.

In the late summer of 2021 after Katherine finished building our eight raised beds and we realized we accidentally ordered triple the amount of soil needed to fill those beds, I reached out to our community garden to see if they could use our surplus. The garden's primary farmer, Sarah, answered the call. She pulled up in a truck with two barrels, her husband and her daughter in tow, to take the extra soil for the community garden. Worms weaved between chunks of sediment as River and Oak bounced between digging, dumping, and playing with Sarah's young daughter. When the new beds at the community garden were filled with the soil, and our French radishes were planted in our own backyard beds, we visited the community garden to see the work the shared soil was doing. Besides the land, the gift of a small, already-created farm nearby convinced me that this town was the place where I should create the Mae House. We exited our house with bare toes, feeling the splits of old porch wood between seams. Our shoes waited for us on the overgrown grass. We slipped them on one by one, grabbed a basket, and made our way to the town's small and mighty community farm. On our walk, the cascading Catskill Mountains remained in the distance, getting closer with each inch. The sun bent low on our 'fros, and the hair on my children's backs got slick with sweat every step we took.

Although community gardens have become pulpits for activism, for people like me, my siblings, my aunts, uncles, cousins, grandmother, great-aunts

and -uncles, they have been the life force of mutual aid and healing within ourselves and others since we can remember. It is the groundwork for what Linda
Goode Bryant so reverently says, "Use what we have to create what we need."
Back at the community garden upstate, the kids weaved through four-foot-high
beds like colorful alleys, sniffing shishitos, tomatillos, and cayenne peppers. A
diaspora of produce colors collect in pockets made from the bottoms of their
filthy T-shirts—because the basket is too much to use, they claimed. I watched
as their bitten fingers de-weeded between the beds as they saw what else was
almost ready for picking for our dinner soon. I have noticed that the plants so
easily survive the two-hour train ride to the city, the thirty-minute subway ride
to Brooklyn, and one overnight in our refrigerator before finding their rightful
homes in the bellies of those we love.

I remain an optimist. The story of the plants, whether we plant them or live
off of them, encourages us to take heed in the process. They whisper: *Slow down
and watch things grow. Share your seeds. Remember your elders. Leave them for the
future who may know better and tend with care.*

I take solace in the plants sown by hands in concrete cities like New York.
Or the rooftop grange my daughter, at age five, attended one summer for a
free camp with other children, where she learned how to naturally tie-dye her
favorite shirt out of vegetables she picked. And in the installation at the hands
of Linda Goode Bryant in Belmont and Brownsville, and in *One Love*, a group of
radical individuals my children and I have joined to gather healthy food to do-
nate to community fridges, with dignity and respect. The ability and availability
for folks to create an oasis out of their two-room apartments and share with
others is never lost on me. I gather these collective images as tokens of ways we
inevitably return to ourselves and people before us. I gather them and I learn and
become braver, too. I gather and I teach my children, who are more often than
not teaching me.

My daughter is nearly taller than I am now. It becomes more difficult to assess the scale of that growth every day. We blink and they're grown, unlike the plant presents I've given to new mothers; a plant's size is more easily charted. Plants no longer grow on sills—they launch over rooms and bead across pre-war living room corners. However, the original thoughtful beauty, the taking note of time in such a way, remains the same. Instead of watching this gift of the earth grow with the babies, the babies grow, the babies pick, and then the babies watch the gift become and live.

Homegoings

Everybody who accomplishes anything leaves home. This action, leaving home, has an effect on the people left behind and sometimes, most dramatically, on the new people one meets.

—JAMAICA KINCAID

t took me three days to remove the olive-green curtain from the rod it called home at the Mae House. The rod was a basic kind that you can find pretty much anywhere: white, steel, with a covering of enamel. The curtain that replaced the olive polyester one was lace. It wasn't the kind of lace worth mentioning; it had no history, no story of being passed down to me from one person or the next. In truth, it was a faux lace I bought in 2012 at IKEA for the bay windows in our Brooklyn apartment. The windows were the only entry source for light into the oval-shaped living room, with a railroad-style dining room, bedroom, and hallway that led to our kitchen, bathroom, and our primary bedroom. I loved the apartment, but there isn't much one can do in a rental with such grim design choices.

The gentle lace that resembles a Victorian rose garden helped, though. It doesn't look like the roses that once occupied my Brooklyn backyard or the ones that grow on the iron stoop railings belonging to Bedford-Stuyvesant's brownstones. I am not entirely sure which room of my grandmother's old Prospect Heights apartment lace curtains once lived in, but I remember them there. Her bedroom, maybe. It was summer. Her armoire was near the window, her room was full of old things: an old couch, pins of Jesse Jackson and Al Sharpton in ornate vintage ring bowls, a dresser with perfume bottles, knickknacks, and a lace fabric runner, too.

In my Brooklyn apartment, one panel of lace did the surprising work of two on one window. The curtain seamlessly blew in the wind and didn't obstruct the light that the bay windows and architecture worked so well to create. I purchased another two panels to hang in each of my bedroom windows. The bedroom received less light, but with the windows open overlooking our landlord's yard, with a fern sitting on the sill, accompanied by a chair and my grandmother's pale blue floral hatbox, the room opened to a past space in time. It was a place I thought I didn't know as this new adult version of me—no longer a kid of Brooklyn, and with a child of her own. But I clearly did know, because of how familiar the space felt.

According to NPR, "In 2019, the Black homeownership rate was about as low as in the 1960s, when private race-based discrimination was legal." The station shared the story of DonnaLee Norrington, a woman who had a dream of owning a home in south Los Angeles. In the house she now owns, three generations of her family call it home, too. The rarity of the purchase may be the single opportunity that pushes not only DonnaLee but her children and their children above the poverty line. "Over the last 15 years, Black homeownership has declined more dramatically than for any other racial or ethnic group in the United States," NPR noted in the same piece that aimed to highlight the racist architecture of the United States.

I read DonnaLee's story one afternoon at my desk in between fifty emails with my housing lawyer. I thought of the deep significance of what I may have given my children and myself at thirty-two—a home owned upstate—right before being told we also had to move out of our rented apartment in Brooklyn. The situation was made more complex by my own thirty-year mortgage that now belongs to Fannie Mae (a common yet limited protected path that is the direct result of the 2009 recession), thoughts of redlining, and the memory of my own mother purchasing a home she did not keep, when she was around the age I am now. What followed after my mother's home purchase were moves by choice and by force, from Maryland, to Long Island, to Virginia, and back to New York City, a long history of the difficulty Black women face in the country just to get *free*. Just to get their children free.

The cycle of attaining and then disenfranchising is not new. Power-hungry New York icon Robert Moses, who nearly single-handedly uprooted entire Black and brown communities in the early to mid-1900s and created generations of displacement, attempted quite successfully to segregate communities of New

Yorkers. For decades, Moses had been lauded for bringing our city into the modern world. Says *The Guardian*, when dissecting Robert Caro's book *The Power Broker*, which is based on the work of Robert Moses:

> Caro shows how Moses transformed New York in ways both progressive and backward, benign and cruel. Many of the slums he removed were horrendous, and their residents got better homes; he really did break the power of Long Island's robber-baron estate owners, finally permitting hundreds of thousands of cooped-up middle-income New Yorkers to drive to the beach at weekends. Then again, he so hated the idea of poor people lowering the tone at the seaside that he built bridges over his parkways with insufficient headroom for buses, so only cars could make the trip. Convinced that African Americans had a special dislike of cold water, Caro alleges, Moses kept temperatures in one Harlem pool deliberately low to keep them away.

However, like many grand forward pushes in the name of modernization (and, ultimately, erasure), there were simultaneous thrusts backward. Notably, activist Jane Jacobs was accused in 1968 of second-degree riot and criminal mischief as she and a group of activists successfully protested a highway that would rip apart the tight-knit community of Greenwich Village in New York City. Despite the work of Jacobs and countless other community activists, the vast landscape of difficulty when it comes to Black and brown renting is unchanged.

"Good morning, Latonya, I hope you are doing well. You will be receiving shortly in the mail the Ninety (90) day notice of termination. But please find a copy now. Thank you and have a nice day." Thirty days after signing my bubbly signature on about fifty sheets of twelve-point Times New Roman papers to close out the purchase of my first home, I received a misspelled text from an uncategorized number stating that I had ninety days to vacate my current apartment in Brooklyn. Although I had the house now, it was never the plan, nor conceivable, to move myself and my children to it full-time. The schools on that side of the river proved to mirror a previous time of life, one that would not adapt (even now with slow neighborhood diversity) for two brown city kids who knew more about egalitarianism than many. The single sought-after private school was not only too high in cost (calling in families who had two or three Teslas at their disposal) but lacked the varied and influential high-level public school education under a Black women–led leadership (however singular) my children received since pre-K in Brooklyn. I knew right away that I would be dealing with court papers that were improperly delivered and incorrectly addressed, and a person who didn't take into account the landscape and difficulty of potential eviction for a mother with two children—difficulty for them as well as for us. I assumed that my Black landlord's daughter, who was handling the building's sale all the way from Montreal, thought I would just leave. That I wouldn't carry the spirit of my own grandmother who refused to leave her rent-stabilized apartment on Classon Avenue in Brooklyn, until she was relocated and promised an apartment back in the original building, or even the childhood version of myself that is no stranger to the eviction process. They thought I would go gracefully and without incident.

It would take one year of attempted negotiations, handfuls of nonsensical incorrect servicing, four unnecessary court dates—two in which I showed and they did not—and six or seven avenues of harassment for a settlement to take place. "We're going to say you're fully paid out. And we're done," the court attorney finally said with a certain kind of jovial and no-bullshit tone that comforted and vindicated me. He was solemn, making me aware that although my case felt singular, it was one of many similar cases in New York City at that moment. However unique I felt, I was just one in a fiery system of folks affected by the pandemic and many who were not, but still were up against the irrefutable money grab and conversion of multiunit buildings to single-family homes where displacement was, in fact, "business as usual." Through time, I had learned, New York City had effectively squeezed out the middle class—leaving many of us unable to afford even the "middle income" that they've set in several million-dollar buildups.

In the evenings leading up to the settlement, I joked with friends that if there was a hell, it was in fact located at the housing court at 141 Livingston Street in downtown Brooklyn. My therapist challenged me to find the part of myself that responded to the trigger of being on the fringes (however false, because of the house I just purchased). "What does it look like?" she asked, and when I responded that it looked like me, she gently prodded further: "How old is she?"

I responded in near hypnosis, "Fourteen, I think."

She nodded. "Can you update her? That this isn't your childhood?" she continued, until the younger part of myself stared back at me with a neck twist and amazement at how time and the mind could feel disjointed and cooperative at once.

In these sessions, my memory is at its clearest. Room for fog no longer exists. Quite often, people who grew up with trauma become storytellers despite that fogginess as we attempt to frame the narrative that is at once created in the mind and in the body. It wasn't until my own impending eviction and settlement as an adult that the struggle to wrap my head around our family's constant movement during my childhood became clear. I realized that the locations and the seasons of my childhood and my children's childhoods intertwined as one abstract picture, and as a result, I was finally able to begin processing without judgment. I could forgive myself and others—and even the system itself, to an extent, for what it did to us. Through storytelling within a native landscape to myself and my children, a new story took shape.

From 1971 to 1997, researcher Roger Webb collected data on almost every single child in Denmark to see if and what effect adolescent moves had not only on childhood but on middle-age adulthood. At least 37 percent of children in his study moved homes at least once. Those who did showed little, if any, adverse side effects to the move. The children who moved multiple times between the ages of twelve and fourteen showed an elevated risk of unnatural mortality and psychiatric disorders.

"I understand you're sad, Oak. I know this is the only home you remember. But the new apartment will make way for new things and new memories, and all of us will breathe easier." Oak had begun to cry when I told the kids our move-out date over dinner at home one evening. I felt for him. I felt for the version of myself that wanted to howl, "It could be worse!" when what he needed was for me to lean in softly. I felt for the tears he shed. I felt the wave of relief and even excitement that set over me as I began to dream about a season with less stress in an apartment that worked better for us. I felt for others who weren't nearly as lucky as we were and are.

"For violent offending, attempted suicide, substance misuse, and unnatural death, there was a sharp spike in risk linked with multiple moves in a year during early/mid-adolescence," Webb found in his research. And the study was even scarier for girls in their teens: "The elevation in violent offending risk was considerably greater in females versus males exposed to residential mobility at age 14 years." For every move during the most delicate fragment of a girl's life, her risk of drug use—and worse, suicide—grew. Of course, Webb explains that the study fails to examine *why* children moved across municipal boundaries to begin with. Familial stressors like dissolution and household abuse are not accounted for, nor is their socioeconomic status. And there was another rip in the thread of the research: children were no longer registered in the study beyond the age of fifteen. Any mediation that may have happened to these children post-study failed to be examined. But even taking into account the flaws in the study's design, the impact from multiple moves for children was confounding. Webb and his colleagues allude that Denmark in particular—a country that keeps a uniquely tight count of its community households and their movements—may have a better way to solve these issues. In Western countries like the United States, moves aren't nearly as closely examined, although the United States has been a mobile society for generations. Webb's study, for example, points to the 11 percent of Americans who moved in 2014.

In 2020, despite chatter about mass exodus from cities like New York, migrations across the United States were fewer than those across the country in 2019. According to the census, in fact, it showed the lowest amount of movement of all the years of available data, reaching back to 1948.

In 2020, people didn't go far. They populated different communities in their region that promised lower rent, more space, and better places to weather the economic storm. While New York City remained quiet, and I imagined a plethora of empty apartments with dancing mice having the time of their lives, the reality was that there were hardly any of these vacated homes. For every one hundred move-outs in NYC, eighty-four others moved in. This pattern was seen across dense states like New Jersey and California, too. Right before the pandemic hit, my neighbors, a lesbian couple with a toddler, went out to the Midwest to see their family and close on an old house they'd always dreamed of buying. After years of looking for something in the city, *home* felt farther from the city. More accessible, too. But after seeing their house and signing their papers, they never came back. A then-unknown virus descended upon their beloved city, and the plane back to pack up and say goodbye to their friends looked like the least of all viable options.

The lace curtain has remained upstate in the Mae House, though it is not in use. We swapped it out with four panels of heavy, hand-sewn curtains I bought for two dollars at a local vintage store from three elderly women at the register. The curtains have dense lace as the top layer, under yards of fabric that feels heavier than my body. The original lace panel brought back from the city is tucked away on the top shelf of the gray room, "the Healing Room," as we call it. Guests visit and shower the room with congratulations, unaware of the fight back in New York City and my very own need for healing.

"At least we get to say goodbye," I said to River and Oak as I untwisted the bamboo shades from their S-hooks that claimed our apartment windows. The shades didn't belong to me; they belonged to Karyn, who lived here before we did. But I loved them so much, so I kept them over the last five years and took them with me for the journey ahead, too.

"Mark the boxes with the things you want to unpack first. Put the clothes and toys that you'd like to use soonest in a black plastic bag." That is what I recall hearing as a kid. My family was facing an impending eviction, and we were living in the suburbs of Maryland. I had barely gotten used to the idea of a house of that magnitude: two floors, a front lawn, a two-car garage, a cul-de-sac with a white house and untreated wood stoops. I had my own room, and there was a deck with a forested backyard that led to a narrow stretch of road behind a copse of trees. In the early mornings, I would catch the direct gaze of a deer in the middle of the road, unwilling to walk toward me or turn around. Eventually, I'd yell, "*Boo!*" or move a little closer so it would become aware of who was actually in charge and trot along. But in truth, I knew that I was more afraid of it than it was of me—scared of how close it might come or what car might emerge and crash into its red summer coat.

That eviction was neither our family's first nor the last. But it was the worst. I was too old to be spared from the violence of disruption and the brittle movement and dance with avoiding reality, despite the fact that your panties may be on the street when you arrive home. My mother was out of work; she had quit in hopes of one or two of her creative jobs being able to provide a roof over our heads. This failed to materialize. Back then, I was an ardent supporter of hers, unaware of the mechanics of financial insecurity. But the thing about my mom was that—*is* that—she is brilliant. The kind of brilliant that oozes out of her fingers. If there was ever a person who could convince you that things would be provided, the world would pull through, and in that event, the house she just rented wasn't too expensive after all, she could. At the same time, she was so generous with her thinking that it wasn't just about her being successful. It was the idea that any woman could do it, too. My mother also wasn't the kind of person you question. Her stories of childhood fistfights between moving subway cars and life as the protector of her own siblings and mother, to some extent, made her the end-all and be-all.

There was a patch of time wherein I was not only frustrated by my mother's choices but wholeheartedly angered by her frivolousness. The kind of angry that only arrives when you have your own apartment and newborn baby, and you would lick, piss, or ho on a corner to pay for the apartment she dozes off in at night. As time stretched on, my relationship to my mother's choices unbounded into empathy. Should she have been so financially insecure to begin with? My father lived somewhere else scot-free. They were no longer married, and child support seemed akin to hitting the lottery. When it came, I presumed it was mine to shop with, rather than the promise of one more day in our home.

It is hard to speak about eviction as part of life's formula if you've spent your childhood and teenage years pretending like they never happened. I was one of those teens that Webb alluded to in his study. At fourteen, with steady friends and unstable living, the performance of stability was murky. At fourteen, the opportunity to share about what's happening at home doesn't arrive in casual conversations at lunch or with a teacher. At sixteen, there's more room within kinship for such topics, a proximity to adultness to make sharing feel more possible. But fourteen is different. It is an undeniable era of lying straight through your teeth to hide the zit or the menstruation blood that leaked through your cotton underwear in biology class—let alone the consequences of your mother's finances, her inability to provide fully to the forces at power. Although not fully understandable, eviction is tangible when folded between the movement of your body in and out of spaces. And it exists as a privacy window at all times.

I had known prior to the eviction in Maryland that home was a strange place. Whether a physical place or a place within your body. We had ended up in Virginia because my great-uncle had decided to leave home and get into his car to drive around, as he did every night. And in that car, accompanied by three of his friends, who he treated like family, he had driven just two blocks away from his mother's home—my great-grandmother's home—when he was killed. Shot, by one of these friends, in the back of his head. He was gone in an instant—a statuesque man of magnitude and force, yanked from where he was most comfortable. Gone and home no longer.

I had known that lights in our house in Central Islip at the time were turned back on after being shut off during my middle school graduation, to which my father miraculously showed up. I had known he asked to use our bathroom and pointed out that the lights were off, that he had pieced together we had been sleeping by candlelight for days. Maybe weeks. I had known that we made it fun, squished together on the floor of the sunroom to keep cool during the summer, ordering Chinese food in the early evening, and sleeping and getting dressed as if it were a great adventure when the sun became our light. I had known how my father treated my mother that day of my graduation. And how I felt as if the lights being off were none of his concern considering he didn't provide anyway.

And I had known that my great-uncle came over sometime later that week. I had always secretly believed that he alone gave my mother the money to turn the lights back on. I had known that he came bearing new shoes for us while my mother was at work. I had known that he acted as a babysitter, walking us to Checkers for lunch and around the block again. Slowly, side by side, like old friends. Or I suppose, like a father. I had known that although he was her uncle—born between a mother and a daughter, pregnant at once—he became my mother's closest friend in age and eternity. I had known that as he walked me around the neighborhood, a neighborhood I had such a fraught relationship with, his black calf-length socks trailed slightly below a four-inch scar on his leg. And I had known, though I don't fully remember, the story he shared of how he got it—a motorcycle and recklessness when he and my mother were much younger. I had known that his scar made me feel seen and was one of the first reasons I began showing off the white-laced speckled spots of vitiligo that took over my knees. I had known that my great-uncle was a big deal: a drug dealer, well respected, powerful, insanely intelligent, and deeply feared. And I had known that my desire to take my own life that summer dissipated just by being talked to so slowly and so carefully by him.

I had not known that months later, he would be dead. A call in the middle of the night, my mother asleep in my brother's room, my sister and I asleep in ours—stretched across white metal beds from one corner of the room to the next, with vintage blankets tucked at our feet and stuffed animals (my favorite moving-eye dolls) hidden under the blankets, because they scared my sister. I had not been able to decipher the indescribable wailing that pierced through my bedroom wall, a thump of a body falling flat on the bedroom floor—my mother, becoming undone. It was the kind of sound that made me jump out of my bed and freeze. Her voice got deeper and higher. She screamed his name again and again like an infant calling for Mama. We ran in and huddled around her while she lay on the floor screaming for him, as if those screams would suddenly bring him back. I have never been able to hear a phone ring in the middle of the night without spiraling into a panic.

In the Pentecostal church where my grandmother was a member our entire childhood, women who pray or who work as collectors, ushers, and kitchen help veil their heads with white lace handkerchiefs. This attachment to the cloth dates back to the literal reading of 1 Corinthians 11:2–16. The delicate lace veil is at once universal, worn across borders, countries, and various sects of Christianity. But in its delicacy, it is also taut—unable to be torn at first or even second attempts—only unstitched intentionally by a slow snip of scissors, undoing the communion of and with it. And lastly, it is ornamental and transparent while remaining wholly recognizable, synthesizing these women and their relationship as warriors of not only God but parishioners of the church in which they fortify their single relationship to Jesus.

My grandmother's Sunday veil was crisscrossed, pinned with brown bobby pins over her golden foam-rolled curls. When we drove to Brooklyn the morning after finding out that my uncle was killed, where lace curtains adorned her own windows and soon her mourning head, my grandmother had said that she already knew. The spirit of her only brother had traveled from Richmond, Virginia, to her apartment in Brooklyn, New York, during her sleep to say a final farewell, where he joined his sister (her sister, and my great-aunt), who died a month after I was born, in her bed during a nap, after complaining of an unrelenting migraine. My uncle visiting my grandmother in her sleep wasn't strange at all. For my entire life, I have believed, and still believe, that my grandmother was otherworldly. She had been known for vivid dreams that were far more in-depth than historical Black matriarchal dreams of fish to indicate someone was secretly with child. She knew almost *too* much, kept it tight, and seemed to float on air. She also had the ability—even through grief—to hold firmly on to a belief in something far greater, far more ordained, than the cards we were given. It was always as if the ground ahead was even more glorious, whether it existed in this world or the next. I bid farewell to my great-uncle with a kiss on his white lace kufi, which covered the new scars on his head. That kiss began our run with several moves across the South.

I carried my grandmother's optimism and my uncle's care with me through our Virginia moves. I overheard my mother's late-night conversations with my grandmother, and I am sure that she fit in a prayer for my mother and for us with each passing day. I held her prayers and those of my mother close throughout the transition and relocation. I decided to name the Mae House after my grandmother, whose profound belief in caring for the homes we keep and the communities we get to be part of has followed me all my life as a map of home when I am lost. Mae is also the middle name I gave to my daughter, River. And May is the month when I signed the papers for the house, and received keys and a deed in response. The signage of the Mae House is deliberate; the words curve like a hug or, when tilted, like a womb, places that held us then and hold us now. In the windows of the art I had created for the house, there are white panels in each room. While it isn't abundantly clear, those white panels signify the lace curtains I hung up and the ones that have followed me through my years. When we moved around, or even when we were steady, my mother would repeat to us, "If you are together, no matter where we sleep, you are home. And we protect each other. *You* protect each other." Although these are words I also feed to my children, I make room for another relationship to home: "As long as you find a way to hold on to something that feels like home, you will make it home."

In Virginia, during the nights we stayed in our car, a hotel, or with my aunt between our houses, I pulled a favorite pillowcase out of my bag to comfort me.

The pillowcase was like a little blanket that often belongs to infants who need help self-soothing at night. It smelled like home wherever and however we got to where we were going next. And as an adult, when my kids see my mysterious pillowcase, they call it my "Night Night." When they see it hidden they yearn for the story of how I became attached to the piece of tattered olive-green cloth to begin with.

When we moved into our new apartment in Brooklyn in the winter of 2023, I packed the pillowcase in my backpack, hoping to shield it not only from the eyes of movers and packers but also from dust and relocation energy. Between my old apartment and my new apartment, we stayed at a friend's plant-filled second-story walk-up for two weeks. The apartment was just three blocks away, and our stay started four days after the case was settled, when I had found a new place I was happy to move us to. I managed to keep the blanket alongside me during our stay at my friend's as a means of solace in the chaos. But once we moved in and I began to unpack my book bag—along with hundreds of boxes to make the new apartment feel like home—I couldn't find the pillowcase anywhere. To this day, it hasn't been found, and I see no sign of it turning up. I don't think it ever will. Or when it does, I don't believe my need for it will be the same.

For generations, Seneca Village, also known as the "Lost Village," was what folks called what we now know as Central Park—specifically, the portion adjacent to the Great Lawn that stretches from West Eighty-third to Eighty-ninth Street. From 1825 to 1857, a group of predominantly Black folks grew one of the first Black and free communities there. Later, writers, historians, and activists alike would argue that the nickname was a misnomer, that Seneca Village was never lost. Like many things, the idealized whitewashing of American history, and more specifically of New York, instead actively chose to bury its existence. The origins of the Seneca Village include a thriving community that also welcomed increasingly marginalized Irish and German immigrants. The village's midwife, Margaret Geery, was even a woman of Irish descent. The Black families who eventually settled there are known to have purchased the land and created their homes in the village as a way to escape not only the overcrowding of Manhattan but the rampant violence and discrimination that occupied it.

"Just as you should know the stratigraphy of the earth and soil occurs, you just know the stratigraphy of people and cultures. You just know that there's something alive and kicking underneath," says public historian Cynthia Copeland as she describes the livelihood of Seneca Village. Those who lived in this expanse of land built structures: three churches (all of which still prevail over 150 years later), barns, stables, two-story homes, and even an all-Black school, Colored School #3. By 1855, half of the Black people living in Seneca Village owned their own homes. To further the debt of discrimination and ultimate power that the free Black community cultivated for themselves, in 1821, New York State required that voters own at least $250 worth of property and hold on to that property for a minimum of three years. By 1845, in the entirety of New York's one hundred eligible voters, ten of them were Blacks who lived in Seneca Village. Within a brief thirty-two years, Black folks were able to create homes, lives, and thriving communities for themselves before being forcibly removed. The government's desire to create public land easily outweighed the private and almost sacred life that this community built. As the development of Central Park grew closer, newspapers and politicians began to describe the villages as "shantytowns." They called the residents "denizens," "squatters," "vagabonds," and "scoundrels." Residents of Seneca Village fought to keep their homes and community intact. But in 1857, the city used eminent domain to remove them. For those who refused: "The supremacy of the law was upheld by the policeman's bludgeons," according to the United States Department of the Interior.

The story of what happened to those who lived in the village is only compounded by the reality that little is known about where they went or the traceable ancestry of the village's residents. In 2011, archeologists began excavation in two primary sites of what was Seneca Village: the yard of resident Nancy Moore, and the home of William G. Wilson, a sexton at All Angels' Episcopal Church. Both were Black. Among the findings in Moore's yard, where original soil remained, were clay pipes, as well as bones from butchered animals. At Wilson's home (where the soil had been dug up and replaced when the new Central Park was built) there were foundational walls, teakettles, and a roasting pan among various artifacts. The most moving discovery was of an infant's shoe, comprised of a leather sole and fabric upper, illustrating the intimacy of life in Seneca Village decades later. As a teary archeological student told *The New York Times*, "The shoe fit someone who walked around here." We know a minuscule portion of what they left behind, and I can't help but wonder about the stories and artifacts they managed to bring with them wherever they made home next.

The first time I flew out of the country to Paris in 2017, I felt the levity of being suspended between spaces. The entirety of the trip surprisingly and somewhat inevitably reconnected me not only to the little things I've carried with me throughout life to create home, but to the idea of *homegoing*, as a layered exploration back to my ancestors and to myself. Flying, for the most part, was something many of my immediate ancestors never experienced. It was not only the slow, elevator-like sensation during takeoff that brought on this feeling but also the entry into another country, wherein my body became unintentionally othered—or in some cases, found.

I often return to a story told to me by activist and artist Sonya Renee Taylor, whom I met a few months into the pandemic. Her permanent Global Impact Visa for the island of Aotearoa was accepted—arguably, one of the most difficult visas to attain because of New Zealand's stringent rules and low acceptance rates from every country. Outside of this tangible win, Sonya's words on how she found her home were the most acute: "I found love and family and heartbreak and ancestors

and healing and a shattering of illusions. Aotearoa wanted to give me what I kept giving away. It gave me myself, and it is within myself that I have discovered the truth home, and it is from that truth that I was free to choose what I desired to add to this palatial estate called myself, and I wanted to add New Zealand to my home."

When I flew to Paris for the first time during the summer of 2017, I had been in the midst of the difficult dissolution of my marriage, which caused me to lose twenty-five pounds in two months. I was trying to navigate my way through it all, particularly what it meant for our living situation—even discussing with my ex about a way of not only sharing an apartment together (although no longer romantically linked) but also sharing a life as a restructured family, if he wished.

I arrived in Paris with the ink barely dry on my first book, *Woman of Color*. It was also James Baldwin's birthday, and like many of my travels from Brooklyn to Berlin in the years since, where I have leaned on the gait of Audre Lorde, Paris provided the cliché that it often does for Black writers. I went looking, and I ultimately found, a berm between these ancestors and me. Ancestors, who also wanted and needed to be in this foreign expanse as a way to acquire some other kind of *freedom*. In my desire for this particular intimacy, I read Baldwin's essay "Equal in Paris" as he chronicled the winter of 1949 when he was accused of and arrested for stealing hotel bedsheets (he had no idea the sheets were actually stolen by a white American friend). On the rue de Navarin, I sat at vintage iron bistro tables, secondhand cigarette smoke fastening to my golden 'fro, and read with fury about his time spent in jail—three or four days sleeping on wood pallets with thin blankets turned into weeks, until it was Christmas, and there he still remained. After several encounters and misrepresentation, the case was eventually dismissed. Baldwin gathered,

> The story of the *drap de lit*, finally told, caused great merriment in
> the courtroom whereupon my friend decided that the French were

"great." I was chilled by their merriment, even though it was meant to warm me. It could only remind me of the laughter I had often heard at home, laughter which I had sometimes deliberately elicited. This laughter is the laughter of those who consider themselves to be at safe remove from all the wretched, for whom the pain of the living is not real. I had heard it so often in my native land that I had resolved to find a place where I would never hear it any more. In some deep, black, stony, and liberating way, my life, in my own eyes, began during that first year in Paris, when it was borne in on me that this laughter is universal and never can be stilled.

After his revelation that only led to my own, I lay in my corner room in Le Marais overlooking the building's garden. Across from my feet, there was a cracked window and a box full of flowers I couldn't name, and one single panel of French lace curtain moving with the wind. It was there that I experienced an unrelenting feeling of roundedness and familiarity. I often return to the notes I wrote in my phone at 2:32 in the morning when I was too jet-lagged to sleep: "I lay in the bed, the lace curtain blowing in, the glass chandelier floating above. I go back and forth between thinking of how this apartment reminds me of my grand-mother, it 'feels' like her. It just does. It is odd."

As I journeyed on my own home-buying process for the Mae House, the meaning of the research I was unconsciously conducting by traveling from Paris to Brooklyn and Brooklyn to Berlin in the short span of four years became trans-parent. The movement of my body forcefully as a child and by choice as an adult became unwanted and wanted tutorials, respectively. The spirit of purchasing my own land in a small village two hours outside of the city was in part a means to challenge struggles and disgruntled relationships of my past and the identi-fication of home. I thought of not only the sweet white mulberries my children could collect in their palms and eat off the tree but the terrain that needed care and that could grow as a free residency space for BIPOC visitors who found themselves seeking similar and brief safety from the post-Covid residents and room for their art. I bought the house for its bathrooms, plentiful garden beds that needed edging, and biodiverse planting with sweet wildflowers that Oak gathers in mason jars, its wide-planked wood floors that River loves to stretch along. But mostly, I bought it for everyone who came before me and the systems and structures that so often try to negate our proprietorship by way of endless redlining and insistent historical erasure.

"Hmm, I think I like that. What do you think, River?" I asked as I placed the lace tablecloth on our wooden table. I had gotten rid of two of the chairs that used to gather around it and began hunting for used other ones to replace them. Boxes overwhelmed our new apartment at every corner. Although each of the kids gained their own bedroom and a bathroom in our new apartment in the city, there were no closets, so I would need to build up and out. The tablecloth was wrapped in a plastic zippered bag that once held my grandmother's ornaments, the kind of zippered vinyl bag that duvets and comforters arrive in on the counter at Macy's. The bag was my grandmother's as well, but I used it for keeping the things I most cared for safe from closet moths. There were holes in the lace, not from the moths but from use and time. Pale brown coffee-like stains sprinkled throughout. I found it at the local Goodwill when I was pregnant with River while rummaging for clothes in 2011, and only took it out of its plastic home on special occasions like Thanksgiving and Christmas. Finally exhaling after a year like the one we'd had seemed like a fitting occasion. River and I twisted the tablecloth until it was perfectly centered. That evening, I climbed up on the chair and hung the Japanese paper lantern that once hung in our kitchen above the bistro table.

Before we had our first meal on the tablecloth in the Mae House, friends brought two bottles of orange wine and a bouquet of dried flowers. A bowl of fruit moved along the tablecloth, looking for its new home, a home that wouldn't take away from the magnitude of the lace. Soon, it was placed on top of the fridge, where oranges and bananas would run over, only to be brought back to the table. Days went on, and my family gathered around the table by candlelight, still with boxes, cable cords, and remnants of what was all around us. Save the tablecloth, nothing was where it should have been; but everything was exactly where it was meant to be.

Field Notes

Let me wear the day
Well so when it reaches you
You will enjoy it.

—SONIA SANCHEZ

The Clock

For the past few months, I have been waking up twice: at 4:00 A.M. when the sky is still dark and even the cats are quiet; and again, or fully, at 11:11, in the late morning. This is when I glance at the clock on the oven, fridge, or on my phone and begin to track how time moves in unison with my body. Waking up late indicates the morning clouds have cleared and my stride has begun. It is a glorious awakening, as if led into the day by an angel. Not like at four, when I wake up in a near sink-full of sweat in my bed and mattress, totally unaware of what day it actually is. At four, I wake up terrified, as if my body has done something awful, and for a good twenty minutes, as I gulp water while it drips from the sides of my mouth, I try to track what disrupted me.

Some evenings, I have the foresight to leave a pencil and paper beside my bed. Other times, I use the notes app in my phone. I wish I could say these notes I scribble or type upon waking make sense. They do not. But I have uncovered that this panic began as I started paying my mortgage at the Mae House, and when I retained a lawyer for the apartment in Brooklyn. Now my sleep gets caught on something, like a dream catcher, but I wake in the nightmare.

Analyzing this has left me more exhausted than the constant waking. Because home is not *supposed* to be in the objects. The clock, for better or worse, is how we mark our days. When Oak wakes, he runs to the fridge to see how long he has slept. In the evening, River checks the smallest purple watch on her desk to count the minutes until her bedtime. A home may not need walls, but memory, rest, and relief rely on the objects. Home is composited within us and the many who were here before us. As a mother, my clean-up process has been in telling my children that the people, the stuffies, tubs of nail polish, wooden train blocks, and their beloved cats will be there when they wake.

I exit the room and make my way to the living room, to close the curtains in the front window. I stand in it, as I do most evenings, looking out, running my fingers across the raised thin white and gray ripped cotton ends. I look at this place I've called home most of my life, the border of here and there. My neighbors across the street who live on the ground floor never close their curtains. But if I stand in my window long enough, it gets darker and the city sees me. And I see it, too, through memories like pictures hung on walls.

September 19, 2020, a crowd of people swarm the street, barricading traffic with their bodies, with their hands, shouting, "Hands up! Don't shoot!"

I remember this.

The Place

It was a sweltering day, and I had walked from Clinton Hill to downtown Brooklyn to meet a friend who just had her third baby. The occasion was a march, and it began to rain as I walked uphill past towers that promised three months of free rent; and then past Whitman housing projects, which less overtly promised a plethora of brown folk, consequential housing, and police activity.

Fort Greene was the place my great-great-grandmother first called home when she moved from the South. It had its own Harlem Renaissance in the 1980s and '90s. In the 1890s, there was a historical uproar when a house sale on Fort Greene Place disrupted the illusions of comfort and class for white folks living in the area.

> Hiram S. Thomas was an unqualified success. He had been born a free man in Drummondville, Ontario, in 1837. He was a college graduate, and during the Ulysses S. Grant administration, in the 1870s, he was the steward of the Capitol Club, in Washington, D.C.

By the 1880s, he had relocated to the popular and prosperous town of Saratoga Springs, one of the posh resort towns in the Adirondack Mountains, a favorite vacation destination of the rich and well-connected of New York City during the Gilded Age. The local Brooklyn paper, *The Brownstoner*, wrote:

> In 1894, while talking with guests at his Lake House restaurant in Saratoga Springs, Hiram Thomas ran into General Edward Molineaux, once a member of General Grant's staff, and a customer from Thomas' days in D.C. Upon hearing that the general was from Brooklyn, Thomas asked him about a property that he had just contracted to buy, on a little street called Fort Greene Place. To his great surprise, General Molineaux lived on that very block, down the street at No. 117! Well, the general told his sister, who told her husband, who told his landlady, Doctor Emma Onderdock. She owned several buildings in the neighborhood and on that block, including the house next door to Mr. Thomas' new building. The good doctor, who had the distinction of being one of Brooklyn's first female doctors, was the main instigator of the furor that followed.

I've watched over the years as the seas of Afros in the park and dinners at Madiba were replaced with coffee lines of white folks and dogs. Madiba closed. Bad business deal, they said. I have been waiting near years for the new fancy pizza shop with a cherrywood awning to open for nights out. I secretly hope the teenagers from MS 113 never stop spending their parents' money at Mario's. The decrease in the Black population in Fort Greene is not only seen, it is duly noted by NYU's Furman Center: In 2000, the Black population in the neighborhood was 41.8 percent. In 2017, it dropped to an astonishing 25.8 percent. I am certain it's much lower this year.

The Jaguar

When I was young, my mother had a black porcelain Jaguar on her rectangular couch table. It was the kind of object she was known for—something unfit to live among not one but five children, and incredibly original. Just like we knew we could not sit on the white couch, we knew we could not touch the jaguar. That didn't stop us. One day during our secret play hours while my mom was at work, my sister and I acted as if the jaguar were a wild animal galloping across the table, from one corner to the next, until it fell off the table to the floor. SMASH!

We both looked at each other, expecting the other to pick it up. Then my sister began to cry.

We started to pick up the pieces, one by one, gathering them in our small palms, being careful not to slice our hands open, which would have simply turned one drama into the next. We found superglue and slowly pieced the jaguar together like a large puzzle. We held it in place until it dried and our fingers were lodged together.

"She won't notice," I said, and rotated it to make sure the seams were nearly invisible and out of our mom's line of vision.

For months, my mother would look with a tilted head from across the room at the jaguar, as if the whole room had changed. And then she began shifting it to optimize its best side, too.

"Hmm, I wonder when that happened," she finally said one day as she noticed the faintest white crack. Every so often, from afar, I would look at it, too. I swore myself to secrecy, that I would never tell what happened.

I still haven't yet.

Mommy, I broke the jaguar. We pieced it back together.

The People

My friend Christy just moved into their new home in New Rochelle, in the suburbs of Manhattan, with their partner and three kids. It is a different sort of place than Christy lived nearly a year ago. In the old place, an orange sofa that I purchased from a friend who moved from California to New York and couldn't fit in their living room sat for two years. Christy left the sofa and apartment behind after getting Covid and spending nearly eight weeks away from their daughter, Ava. It took four Covid tests at the hospital during the early days of the pandemic for Christy to be reunited with their daughter, only to move out of New York City to create a new home with their family in the South. Once there, Christy proposed to their partner on Juneteenth in their kitchen. They found home in this joy and the memories of that temporary Southern space, but it could not be a true home for them because they could not be themselves—and so they made their way back to New York.

It is the evening of the harvest moon; the transition from summer into fall is imminent. I am bewildered by how everyone in the world sees the same moon at different times. On Sunday, upstate, the moon looked as if it were sitting atop a mountain near our house. "We could almost reach out of windows and hold it in our hands!" the kids yelled. I cried at the sight of it.

In Brooklyn, I walked up the hill and saw the moon hanging between two streets and above my favorite brownstone, the pink sky illuminating it. I wrote Christy that night from the kitchen to check in, as we often do as the season transitions. In the morning, at 6:00 A.M., an hour before I was awake, a time Christy takes for themself to pray, dance, write, and even listen to old R&B, they wrote me back:

You know, when you're a child of immigrants, and a child of the African diaspora, you're introduced in the beginning to the hindrance to achieve freedom, seeking shelter, and assembling and constructing a home for your future. I never dreamed to look over the walls and chain-link fence America built around my family, my identity, or my personhood.

My mother's deportation back to her home country of Jamaica disrupted our comfort, her old home had become foreign after 35 years of playing the role of an exceptional American, working, and dreaming. Like you, like all of us.

Everything I thought was home began to blister. The roots that I trusted were pulled from the ground, ones my mother planted in New York with wisdom, love, ginger tea, and warm rice and peas. I never thought to question the bed she planted her seeds in.

Then the start of the 2020 pandemic, I was diagnosed with uncertainty. COVID-19 is a disease that doesn't quite disappear—it's an agonizing disaster.

I no longer felt safe after recovery, my roof became too heavy to hold up, it suddenly vanished, terrified of separation repeating.

I had my daughter in tow, on my journey of discovering placement, love, empathy, and financial security.

I wondered if the feelings of fear, excitement, and guilt were similar feelings my mother carried when she migrated to America with my siblings under her arms.

I thought to think like her, always ahead of the game. To make moves that will change me. I confronted truths I've been told to bury in the past. I knew my return to New York would be our return. New York has a way of centering itself in your heart forever. It can go unnoticed until you walk away.

I was nervous for my partner. As searching for my home as a gay woman is a fight, this isn't an unusual obstacle. It is just one that is scary. The more I parent my daughter with honesty, and provide her with choice, towards herself, and what our home should look like, I do my best to gift her with what my world hasn't extended to me. I have to convince society that my identity is deserving of warmth and protection. That my gender deserves to be questioned, that conforming can contribute to a loss of self.

Self-discovery is a lesson; home is where I go, therefore it can never erupt, as I'm planting the leftover seeds my mother left me, sowing them in the ground while we mourn displacement, yet celebrate the home I am making as a Black lesbian and as a parent, an artist, and as a lover.

My paintings found new walls, and my sofa is where a hairbrush and grease sit beside me while I braid my daughter's hair, and sweet ginger tea brewing for all of us on the stove.

Orphaned in New York, and with a home.

Can you believe it?

This life of transition is not limited to Christy. That night, a news alert: *1140 Afghans expected to find refuge in New York. 240 in New York City.* The dizzying questions on everyone's minds: Where? When? How will they assimilate?

Soon after, more news on my phone: Haitians who have spent years in South America with children who do not speak creole are carried on the bare backs of their mothers and fathers. They are detained at the border town of Del Rio, Texas, photographs of them being grabbed by border patrol on horses, and instead of the reception and protection they believed they would receive, they were deported, with a lack of lawyers and little to no conversation. The laws that would protect them expired on July 29, 2021. They are now forced to create new homes in their mother country—a country they do not know—lives that lack basic access to food and shelter, lives lived under acts of violence only understood in the last few weeks because of an earthquake and the assassination of their prime minister.

Later, I turn on WNYC in anticipation of Brian Lehrer's pragmatic note-taking and research-driven voice, and I am unable to turn off the heart-wrenching news of Rikers Island, where men are forced to make homes within intake, a process that should take no longer than a week. Some are given food and water, thrown at them through iron bars; others hang themselves from those same bars in the process, finding another version of home in heaven or hell, considered a better home than the one a six-foot-by-six-foot cell could offer.

I shut the news off in frustration and read about Kelis's farm in Temecula, California, about two hours outside of Los Angeles. In the piece, Kelis discusses being on tour in Europe when the pandemic hit, then coming back to quickly sell her home with her husband and move to the farm full-time soon after. "I'm as farm as they come," she says to Roxane Gay in *Harper's Bazaar*.

> "You change. I came out here with a completely different idea of
> what was going to happen. I thought I was going to be cute. I really
> thought I was going to have cute farm things . . . [but] that is not
> the case." Kelis has been busy cultivating the property, building
> an outdoor kitchen, and caring for the livestock (more than
> 30 animals, with names like Marvin Gaye, Whitney Houston, and
> Huey P. Newton) along with their Great Pyrenees, Grits, Biscuit, and
> Gravy. Finding her way has taken a combination of research and
> intuition.

The longer I stand in the window, the quicker I lose track of the evening's time. I snap out of my daze and notice the way my snake plant in a boat-shaped aged terra-cotta pot is leaning over the edge of the windowsill next to the corner of the curtain, readying to tip over. I inch it farther back, stabilizing it for the night and, one by one, pull each curtain to the center so that they join together.

The Junk Drawer

Everyone has a junk
drawer. I am convinced,
no matter how neat or
obsessive the person is,
there's one drawer—it
can be slim, wide, deep, or
short—that folks rely on
as a catchall. When I was
a kid, our junk drawer had
it all. It reminded me of
those episodes of *Barney*
I watched from the living
room floor. Barney would
sing, "See what we can
make today, yay!" and pull
out scarves, paper, bikes,
crayons from his magical
bag—whatever he needed
to make something with
his friends. I sat mesmerized in crisscross apple-
sauce, waiting for what he
would dream up.

My childhood junk
drawer had a bottom, of

course—unlike Barney's bag. But we could still find anything we needed, create anything we desired—fold-back clips, gold paper clips, a handful of number two pencils, always one black pen, surely two red ones, a set of keys that no longer had use, nail glue if an emergency should arise, and about twenty dollars nearly exactly in loose change. If something was missing from someplace else in the house, it would be found there. My mother did not bother cleaning it out. Instead, she added to the junk drawer, and this, rather than the object's original intended place, became a reliable part of our existence—just like my favorite blanket or the presence of my siblings. Relying on something to be there when you need it—isn't that the core of a home?

In my home now, I organize the junk drawer. Pencils and pens get wrapped in the rubber bands left over from the stack of mail. There are two woven baskets from the local home store where I put batteries and extra keys. There's a small square box that collects yellow, white, and blue chalk sticks that the kids use to write on the chalkboard across from the drawer: I LOVE YOU, MOMMY! in big letters. Next to the chalkboard, there's a height chart in the doorframe, tracking the kids' growth these last four years. The last one reads:

- May 2021, River, 10
- May 2021, Oak, 6

They have started to sign their own names. The pen I mark their heights with remains in the junk drawer, tucked between the baskets and the cardboard box.

Every time the kids go in there to look for what they need, I follow behind them and tidy it up again, shifting things over, tightening the rubber band around the writing utensils, placing the keys in order of size. No one besides the kids sees the inside of my junk drawer; yet each day, I reorganize it as if the cupboards are going on their own walk around the neighborhood to be judged. This is life at home: we piece together broken bits and reshuffle the mess, even though no one sees it but us.

A Desk of One's Own

Afro-American literature is certainly part of an African tradition. African tradition deals with life as an experience to be lived...We see ourselves as part of a life force; we are joined, for instance, to the air, to the earth. We are part of the whole-life process...And therefore living becomes an experience, rather than a problem, no matter how bad or how painful it may be.

—AUDRE LORDE

"What's the first thing you need done?" Katherine asks. We are on the phone, discussing the Mae House. The question takes me by surprise, and I hesitate. It is April; it has finally stopped raining in Brooklyn, and my apartment is filled with that strange nearly-but-not-quite-summer heat. My proposed closing date for the Mae House had come and gone. The bank needed more paperwork to show that I was still working at the same financial pace I had worked for the previous two years. They cared less if I had the money now, more if the money would continue coming in. I sent pay records and certified letters from my CPA showing that I was one of the fortunate few who were able to stay afloat, the path ahead for me more promising than not. I paid for the house's front steps to be rebuilt to code before my name was on the deed, and I envisioned us in that home before I sent in a deposit. I put my faith in the house and needed the bank to have that same faith in me. I was willing to bet on this vision even before it was fulfilled.

As a vital part of that vision, I needed the people who worked with me to update the house to match the soul of the house itself. It was important that they care about making old things anew, about the story of a place. Katherine was perfect, a single parent and female carpenter introduced to me by a mutual friend. She attended a local community college upstate in the evenings and cared for her kid in the day, while working under a few men already well established in the construction field. She told me that she wanted to inspire women to be able to do these things on their own.

After finally closing, I moved through a handful of sleazy contractors who dropped pallets on my streets instead of my driveway, and I had several small anxiety attacks when realizing that Katherine's words were coming to fruition. I was doing the hard stuff on my own.

I think about her question—what is the first thing I need done—with the phone glued between my shoulder and ear as I swirl in my office chair and chip the red polish off my index finger. I filled the space: "Umm . . . that's a good question."

In truth, the first thing that came to mind was a fence. The one that existed was over a decade old and was nearly black with age. It had succumbed to the lack of care between owners. When the contractor removed the fence from the ground, he shared that it had never been secured with cement to begin with. I told Katherine.

"That's an interesting answer," she responds quietly. "Why is that?"

"I guess, although I'm happy about the house and the space for us, I'm not sure of the people. In the city, I was forced to know my neighbors across the hall. Their religious beliefs and their political ones, too. For the most part, we agreed. And when we did not, we settled on what brought us together; the necessity of closeness."

Surrounded by the beauty of the country, with its quietness and near isolation, figuring out who and what to know isn't as necessary as it is in the city. Upstate was another part of New York that often felt like another part of the country entirely. Building a fence around the Mae House would allow the kids to be outside while simultaneously keeping them close. But enclosing the yard would also create a clear border around what's mine almost immediately, like reaching out to hold your newborn to your chest as soon as it exits your body. Put my baby on my chest, let it feel my flesh. I wanted to roll around my yard butt naked, protected and free to watch the grass grow.

It wasn't just the yard and the fence, though. There was another piece of the house that I felt like I could take a pencil to and mark it as mine somewhere deep. "Oh, and the studio. Well, a desk mostly!" I blurt out.

The garage next to the house is nearly as big as the house itself, with Virginia creepers crawling on its back and poison ivy starting to make its way in the bike casing behind it. It has two floors and one thousand square feet of good beams as bones. It also has a loft and an oversize hay window, which could be opened from the top after removing a four-by-four piece of wood from its latches. A few years back, someone had begun to insulate the space, but presumably stopped when they realized how difficult of a job it would be for just one person with a pipe dream. They added kitchen counters and cabinets on the bottom floor and a tall cabinet that now hosts the several cans of paint waiting to be used on the main portion of the house. There's some kind of pump that was likely used for a wood-burning stove that warmed the room. From the outside, it is just a garage; from the inside, it is someone's half-finished project, waiting years for another person to pick up from where they left off.

In my mind, it is a kitchenette, a daybed layered in cream sheepskin, layers of Moroccan rugs tucked under elephant feet, a cherry-trimmed '70s-style glass table and Eames-inspired chairs to sit in the middle. Upstairs, I see open bleached beams and finished foam insulation, bookshelves with Toni, Sonia, Maya, Joan, Alice, Audre, and Lucille sitting stately. And then there is a large desk, sitting beside the hay window fitted with glass, mirroring the window directly across the room. The desk is lined in Popsicle-stick-size beams of light, streaming from the three skylights that cool the raised ceilings in the summer and heat it with sun in the winter. I see the mountains watching over me, as they surely watched over every other project that once began and ended in this space.

Of all the many projects on the list to create and renovate at the Mae House, it was strange that the studio—more specifically, the desk—became of primary importance to me. For one, the house needed to be renovated quickly to become available as a rental and the BIPOC residency I was planning for. Anyways, much of my writing is done during weekdays, when I would be in Brooklyn. Still, I could almost smell the burning wood rising from the bottom floor or the fresh black coffee I would brew twice-over in the Chemex on that desk next to the books and under the window, with a tarnished silver spoon of honey drip-drip-dripping beside it.

Besides my desk in Brooklyn, my childhood desk was the only other desk I had ever owned, and I had acquired it almost exactly twenty years ago. I close my eyes and there it is, smelling distinctly of thrift store and aged sharpened pencils. It was late summer when it arrived in my bedroom in Fort Washington, Maryland. I had spent the summer on Long Island with my aunt and uncle, fantasizing about dinners with two parents and never having to share anything with four other siblings. I did not want to return home to the South, where my mother had purchased her first home and spent months decorating it. I cried like a baby when summer waned and my days were shortened. The South, for me, was always a point of contention. It didn't matter how beautiful the spaces were or how expansive the parks promised to be—I felt inherently more visible in the South, which only made me feel, in the end, more invisible each year.

My mother caught on to this. "I got you something," she giddily told me as she wrapped me in her arms when I arrived home, the bags from my trip still hanging on my shoulder. As we walked up the steps, through the hallway, and then made the left to my room, my stomach dipped. I stepped through the doorway and gasped. "I *love* it!" A desk filled up the empty corner. It was pastel yellow, lighter than my favorite banana Laffy Taffy candy. It had beige borders and wooden handles, and it arched slightly on each side. It came with a matching mirror and chair.

"I almost got the matching dresser, but I wasn't sure where we would put it," my mom explained. Every part of my body trembled with elation.

My mom told me that she and my father, who had stayed with us for some time, spotted the set at a yard sale as they drove by. I knew my father didn't help purchase it, though my mother would present it otherwise.

"I saw it from the road, and I knew it was so you! Grandma wants to see you at it, too," she went on. My grandmother had been the queen of old things, a collector of the macro and micro, pieces with stories—desks included.

On the left side of the desk, I arranged a colorful collection of nail polish to near perfection. Emory boards were in plastic cups, an oversize Dollar Store bottle of remover next to the mirror. In the drawer, a few pencils, and on the desk, composition books I had already written in. I eased back into the room, my house, my new desk, and my life after that. I even forgot about wanting to stay in New York. There I had been, dragging my feet through the door. And there my mother was, seeing me and what I most needed: room to be me, even at twelve.

In June of 2020, as thousands of protestors barreled down my typically quiet Brooklyn street, I had decided to host storytelling courses to keep me afloat in an isolating time and to create community with women who were all over the world—California, Australia, Georgia, Chicago, and Brooklyn. It wasn't just the pandemic that had stifled our voice; it was the environment, people, and expectations that had performed this silencing for years. My desire to shore up words was as deep as it ever had been. I was on unemployment briefly; my kids were home all day. I wrote sentences in my phone's notes app and cried in the back row of many of those protests until I realized my place this time was at home. Police cars burned with turpentine at intersections. Big businesses padded their storefronts with particleboard. Few conversations were had about the idiocy and aggression of the men in full riot gear marching down my street. The only words I could metabolize were *Black Lives Matter.* New York City felt as if it were exploding at every cross-walk. My thoughts felt as if they were exploding, too.

I could not run away from any of it, nor could I run from the words that were lodged into my brain after reading an interview with Toni Morrison in *The Paris Review*. I read parts of the interview over a dozen times, fitting in bits of Toni's answers that aligned with my life at that moment, stuffing them in my pockets to take with me for the journey. I felt inexplicably tied to this:

> I have an ideal writing routine that I've never experienced, which is to have, say, nine uninterrupted days when I wouldn't have to leave the house or take phone calls. And to have the space—a space where I have huge tables. I end up with this much space [she indicates a small square spot on her desk] everywhere I am, and I can't beat my way out of it. I am reminded of that tiny desk that Emily Dickinson wrote on and I chuckle when I think, Sweet thing, there she was. But that is all any of us have: just this small space and no matter what the filing system or how often you clear it out—life, documents, letters, requests, invitations, invoices just keep going back in.

The interviewer goes on with a lightning round of questions akin to those found in the Dr. Seuss books I've spent years reading to my children.

> Could you write on the bottom of a shoe while riding on a train like Robert Frost? Could you write on an airplane?

Toni responds, "Sometimes something that I was having some trouble with falls into place, a word sequence, say, so I've written on scraps of paper, in hotels on hotel stationery, in automobiles. *If* it arrives, you *know*. If you know it *really* has come, then you *have* to put it down."

I repeated these words to the women in the storytelling workshop. It was urgent. Get words down, the streets are exploding. Yet for an hour, in Zoom meetings where our floating heads shed tears, time was our friend. I was not a teacher, nor was I an editor like Toni Morrison, but I felt this strange calling to quietly connect the grievances of my past self and create room for whatever selves we were building now, together. Twice a week, from my desk, I told the women their stories mattered; twice a week, I reminded myself that not only did mine matter as well, but so did the stories of my children.

"Move your chair closer to your desk, Oak," I requested as I scooted his chest up against the edge of the wooden school desk. It was fall of 2020, and his public school, which started out as hybrid, had gone remote again. The city was unsure of what to do with the uptick in cases. There was a clusterfuck of disagreement between the unions, principals, the city government, and the state.

"Mute your mics!" the kids' teachers said. Houses were turned upside down, mothers spotted in robes, slightly off screen. Oak's nerves were palpable, and tantrums (for me and him) happened like clockwork by two o'clock, followed by physical and emotional withering by five.

The only real saving grace was his desk at home, which looks like his desk at school. The fall before, I had purchased two desks, one for each child, from Amazon. They were a trial, like how when they were in kindergarten, we practiced proper homework evenings. The desks were hugely discounted because they had been made incorrectly—a wobbly screw here, a slanting desktop there. When they arrived, the dings and dents that the site had warned of didn't seem like anything that couldn't be fixed. I purchased a can of dayroom yellow paint from Farrow & Ball and painted two coats on each of the desk's legs. When finished, I placed them side by side under the mural in their room, with their blue IKEA art cart between them so they could each grab what they needed.

River's desk sits beside a six-drawer pale yellow dresser that looks like it could have been from the same set as my childhood desk. We got the dresser for free from our neighbors across the street who were clearing out their house. It stood on the curb, surrounded by baby toys, lamps, and adult clothes. "You sure you don't want to keep this?" I asked them in confusion. "No, no. It's been in our family long enough, and we really aren't using it," they replied. My ex and I carried it into our one-bedroom apartment that day. The drawers were already lined with blue-and-white Con-Tact paper. I filled them with hand towels and reusable napkins, extra clothes that didn't fit inside our makeshift closet. I posted a photo of the dresser on Instagram, and readers began to recall their similar pieces from the '90s. The messages rolled in, so I googled the dresser's origins to see if I could get another one for the kids' room. I found its twin desk, and it looked awfully like the desk I once had, the Laffy Taffy yellow, the curves, the knobs. Could it be the dresser my mother once saw nearly two decades ago and almost picked out for me? To this day, I am unsure, but it felt like it was. As my children sat at their desks doing homework beside the dresser that looked like the one from my childhood, I had no idea that in a year they would be at home working and creating— once, and then again—in the midst of a pandemic. I saw them only as my mother had once seen me. This is the work so many of the Black women and writers I admire discuss: this growing, this creating from spaces, for generations.

One evening recently, a small black book with yellow block lettering arrived at my door. It was wrapped in a single-layer white envelope, stamped *London, 24/08/2021*. I hadn't ordered anything from London, and I surely hadn't done so on the twenty-fourth of August, when I had spent several days upstate measuring walls and texting masons about basement leaks. As the kids watched a movie in the next room, I sat at the kitchen table with a chilled glass of wine and ripped open the package, hoping to unlock the stalled words in my head, hoping to find a way to say what I was feeling. *Black Women Writers at Work*, the book in my hands read. The names of fourteen literary giants graced the cover. A note fell out from inside the cover. It was a gift from my then boyfriend, right on time. I sank into the chair with the kind of relief that arrives only when you're being seen. Some women like gifts of diamonds; for me, old books will do.

The book was written in 1985 and reprinted the year I was born. The author, Claudia Tate, was a celebrated and brilliant literary critic, known as the first scholar to teach Black desire and subjectivity to her audience. Tate taught

readers resistance by considering what resistance meant linguistically, and by being one of few with the ability to critique their creativity. She had conversations with well-known African American writers and women whose work was often overlooked by literary platforming. Her timeless and necessary work *breathes* in this collection. She had passed away in 2002, when I was just thirteen, and I wonder if she—or the women she included in this book—knew her work would nurse so many other Black writers. I cracked open the aged pages, the spine unwilling to stretch apart, for it had been shut for so long. The first conversation that unfolded on my lap was between Tate and Audre Lorde. It is noted in the book that Lorde had preferred that the word *Black* be capitalized throughout the interview. This literary change would not take root across the linguistic economy until some thirty-four years later, as a response to the millions protesting for Black lives. Lorde's conversation with Tate is one of the longest in the book. Simple questions get entire passages as answers:

> I write for myself and my children and for as many people as possible who can read me, who need to hear what I have to say—who need to use what I know. When I say myself, I mean not only the Audre who inhabits my body but all those feisty, incorrigible Black women who insist on standing up and saying "I am and you cannot wipe me out, no matter how irritating I am, how much you fear what I might represent." I write for these women for whom a voice has not yet existed, or whose voices have been silenced . . . My responsibility is to speak the truth as I feel it, and to attempt to speak it with as much precision and beauty as possible.

Oak came crawling in the kitchen begging for a snack. He's the kind of child whose appetite is never satisfied. I say it's because of the open-heart surgery he had when he was five. That is a part of his life that I have been unable to put words to because of the fear that flashes through my mind when I think about it—the rush at my chest knocks me off my feet: him in a hospital bed, us not knowing what would happen next. I have no words in my hands or in my heart for it. I give Oak a small helping of grapes to sustain his sweet tooth and his invisible hunger pangs, and move back to Audre Lorde's words. Claudia Tate asks: "Is writing a way of growing, understanding?"

Lorde continues,

> Yes. I think writing and teaching, child-rearing, digging rocks (which is one of my favorite pastimes), all of the things I do are very much a part of my work. They flow in and out of each other, help to nourish

each other. That's what the whole question of survival and teaching means. That we keep our experience afloat long enough, that we share what we know, so that other people can build upon our experience.

I don't know if I believe everything I said to the women in my storytelling workshop. I tell my children life will return and the work we do every day matters, because that has to be true enough. This is my means of survival. I did not finish college. I had a baby and quit school when River was nearly one, and I had enough credits in writing and literature to eventually transfer to Hunter College, where I could truly focus. But I struggled with math, so much so that it took pulling all-nighters to make sense of the basics of geometry. I can't tell you where a colon or semicolon belongs. I can't tell you how many times I google the words I mean to write to make sure they are the words that I mean. My life as an autodidact is riddled with insecurities and misnomers. However, I make space and envision corners for what I do, because there is little promise if I don't. And if I don't do right for myself, how am I to offer art to my children, the way my mother and all literary mothers did for me?

"Writing makes me feel like I am doing something greater than myself in any given moment. I feel as if I am moving further than anything that may oppress me or ail me," I tell my therapist as I sit at my desk, with a sense of desperate declaration when it comes to parenting while writing. I've been thinking of Virginia Woolf's piece *A Room of One's Own,* trying to connect her struggle to write with my own. In the iconic literary piece, Woolf creates fictional universities and uses metaphors to examine the writing process, and eventually, she lays bare the struggle—the lack of money, respect, and labor—for female writers. Woolf ultimately suggests it is patriarchy that leads to the female communicative absence.

"Women have served all these centuries as looking glasses possessing the magic and delicious power of reflecting the figure of man at twice its natural size."

In a 2019 feature of my Brooklyn apartment on a well-known interior design website, I was asked about the mid-century wooden desk that sat in my living room. I told a story about a friend who found the desk, who felt it was for me; I said we went back to get it together. By omission, I lied about the origins of the desk simply because I feared its place in my home implied that I was a ho for sleeping with someone new a year after my separation, and not self-sufficient, because the desk was that man's idea.

Here is the root of the real story: I had been working on my first book at a café for months. When not at the café, I worked at the dining room table, and the park, and, oftentimes, on the train. All of these places provided me some semblance of peace with my work, but they lacked my identity as a writer. My then partner, a lover and a writer himself, had taken note. "You need a desk of your own. Somewhere you can work. And it needs a place in your home," he said one afternoon, when I sat at his dining room table to just get *one more thing down.* I hadn't read Virginia Woolf's famous piece yet, and I didn't understand the importance of his statement. One evening, he found the desk online, and together, on a brisk, snowy day, where the flakes were fat clusters that soaked my headscarf and his forest-green cap, we picked it up from a gentleman in Park Slope. The man showed us all its weird quirks, caressing the tabletop, almost unwilling to let it go.

"It doesn't like water," he told us. "Are you carrying it out like that?"

Together, we loaded it in the back of a taxi van and then lifted the desk with our knees into my apartment. We found a spot for it next to the fireplace. The light was just right. I could watch the kids from there, too. *I* paid for the desk. I did not sleep for the desk either. But when recounting the origin story of the desk still, I felt I had to withhold, not because of some internal privacy clause but because I knew that judgment would be offered if I told the whole truth, because of a larger outcry in the world of women who write, especially Black women. Thinking I should have the desk was a beautiful and kind gesture from him for me then, and I know now that it in no way lessened my own inherent value.

In contrast to Woolf's work, he was just a man as men should be, placing value in my womanhood. Not one willing to make me subordinate in service of himself, in a field we at some microscopic level share. My desk received me. I received it. Together, we have sought some kind of complex refuge from the details of life.

"This is a red oak slab harvested from the park. The live edge is quite stunning. And if you look here, it has this wonderful symmetry in the curves and art on it." Roger, the owner of the Brooklyn shop, described everything around us as we walked through aisles of harvested pieces of local trees. Some were small, some were large, and they were tucked in a single metal cubicle like slots so you could see them from all sides. Although the trees were dead, they felt alive, waiting for their next lives in someone's home—or possibly in someone's imagined writing room.

"No wonder I'm drawn to this one," I said. "My son's name is Oak."

I told Roger that I had named Oak after the hardiness and strength of the trees. It's all I could think about when I got pregnant. It was a high-risk one, after a late-term loss. I typically don't lay my entire life out within minutes of getting to know someone, but I was warmed by the energy of the space.

"This seems perfect, then," he said. "You can also shorten it and have a few pieces for other things." His soft and caring demeanor made the cost of the slab go down like warm lemon water. Roger and his team would flatten, cut, and belt-sand the slab. The cuts would yield a forty-eight-inch custom cut that would be from the center of the slab so that it would fit the width of my body just right while sitting. The desk wasn't only a sustainable choice, it was one that was centered on keeping the story of my work, but making sure that the power of the room as I most knew it would transfer from Brooklyn to the Hudson Valley. We needed to fill in the grain with epoxy. I purchased four steel legs from Etsy that felt like they would add to its character. Of course, Roger and his team could have done all of this for me—they specialize in creating furniture; but unlike my Brooklyn desk that someone thought up and found for me, the vision of that upstate writing studio was so clear and mine. Its creation needed to fit my imagination, down to the grain—a room, a desk, a life of one's own.

School has begun in Brooklyn, full-time, finally. The bells of the church next to my apartment have started to churn their midday music. This music remains a reminder for me to get up from my desk and stretch my legs. I walk around the apartment, where forgotten sketchbooks from the kids' morning art session greet my feet in the hallway, as if they threw them from their hands when we rushed off to the schoolyard. In Oak's book, there are sentences explaining his art. In River's, half-folded pages reveal collages and pieces of a story she has started in her school's creative writing class. She read a portion of it to me last night, and all I heard was her use of the word *dead*, and then, the cliffhanger, to be continued . . .

I return to my desk and play a little song: the tap-tap on my keyboard, the crunch of my chair, the sweet wood friction of desk drawers going in and out and out and in. A hymn of my own making.

Li'l Red

May you study the pink of yourself. Know yourself riverine and coast. May you taste the fresh and the saltwater of yourself and know what only you can know. May you live in the mouth of the river, meeting place of the tides, may all blessings flow through you.

—ALEXIS PAULINE GUMBS, *UNDROWNED*

After the grayest New York winter I've ever encountered, it was March and the sun was glorious and it didn't feel like fool's spring upstate. It would still be four weeks before the forsythia bloomed in the backyard trap that lined the alley, behind the garage, under the willow tree; three weeks before the first paying guest arrived at the Mae House; two months before the first family came to participate in our Rest as Residency—and I was busy rushing to hide the little red toolbox from the cameraman's lens.

Rest as Residency was a dream revealed to me when I was in the process of buying the house. Taken from my own experience as a child, then later as a single mother in the pandemic sheltering in place in New York City, and finally, the intimate lesson I received when reading botanist Robin Wall Kimmerer's *Braiding Sweetgrass*. Rest as Residency offers Black families a space, the Mae House, to rest for free (and not contingent on their labor). It had stuck with me through the five months of renovation, shuffling between New York City and the tiny town on the train, sometimes for an overnight stay, or sometimes to turn around the same day. With dust still lingering in the air, it is what I considered as my grief-ridden body packed the small red rectangular toolbox with all the tools I purchased for the house and for myself that fall and winter. I wanted to offer to others what I most needed for myself.

The toolbox had to be tucked away before a photo shoot with Farrow & Ball, a luxury, sustainable paint company, with the purpose of documenting the color story in the house. The June before, when the renovation was a pipe dream I wasn't yet sure I could pay for, I walked through the house with a phone a few feet from my face, FaceTiming a color expert, Nicole, from Farrow & Ball's team. Color, and what it evokes emotionally, was an important design objective for the Mae House. Nicole's curls filled the camera, an obvious nod to her identity as a Latina woman. I felt deeply comfortable explaining the point of the house and what I was attempting to translate through the color choices in each room. Through color, one can elicit a range of emotional states. By choosing various colors throughout the room and allowing the objects to be designed alongside those color choices, we are engaging in an exercise that opens the room to interpretation. Farrow & Ball was tired of people choosing various versions of white and claiming creative license. They wanted to highlight the elevation of color in a home and how it sparks stories and translates into time and emotionality.

The Mae House was a perfect canvas, although one that was painstakingly time-consuming. For months, rooms were painted again and again, sometimes in the wrong shade or finish, only to be repainted or touched up right until the night before the photo shoot. The weekend of my color consultation, I purchased the red toolbox from Amazon after spending three weeks searching for one on Etsy. The ones there were mostly oversize, oxidized, green and blue versions that looked hearty and capable, well-loved, but not what I had envisioned. Part of what we desire is often what we imagine. Unlike the fence I knew I needed prior to moving into the house, the toolbox served as an emblem for what I was embarking on, without full acknowledgment of the path or purpose. What was I going to fix with my own two hands anyway? What needed the weight of something heavier, specific—something a paintbrush could not conceal?

There were no framed photos at the house—or nails, for that matter—but the first tool for that red toolbox was a '60s-era Vaughan ball-peen hammer with a splintered handle. The kids and I found it one afternoon, walking in the village, moving from coffee, to lunch, to the house, and back out again for snacks. Popcorn, Popsicles, and encounters with new neighbors landed us on a side street in front of a dilapidated house, where an older gentleman who spent part of his time in the city was cleaning out his home goods and stacking them like *Tetris* pieces inside. For him, there was no difference between what worked and what did not, what was, frankly, gross, and what was a gem waiting to be loved. I could tell it all held meaning that was either conjured or true as the kids and I trailed behind him from room to room. "Oh, that over there . . ." he would begin each sentence while pointing at something seemingly unremarkable.

"Oh, Mommy, look, a piano!" the kids squealed from the back room of the house, cutting him off midsentence.

"Let them take it!" the man proclaimed as he walked alongside me to the room they huddled in. The piano: a dusty Casio keyboard with black electrical tape holding the split base into one piece. "More tape will do the trick to keep it intact."

We left with our hammer and two short-stemmed wineglasses. My children would be banished to playing the keyboard outside on the man's rotting baby-blue deck. On my way out, I spotted four espresso-colored dining chairs, some with docile tan-and-chocolate seat cushions. One had been replaced, another forgotten about entirely. After I purchased them, the gentleman later dropped the chairs off at my front door when his day of selling was over and also brought a broad arrow ratchet screwdriver and a tin of schoolteacher's chalk. Later that evening, the kids wrote *Black Lives Matter* in rainbow block letters on our tiny street. When they were finished writing, they ran in through our red front door, proud of their work and ability to occupy themselves.

"Mommy, you have to come see!" Oak shouted with his right foot holding the screen door.

I walked down our newly replaced, pressure-treated deck, which I would often incorrectly call a *stoop* out of habit. BLACK LIVES MATTER! The kids had written the words in chalk in front of the house. One glance at them and a pit grew in my stomach and crawled up my throat. "We are already Black," I snapped. "We don't need to write it in the middle of the street!" I worried about how our neighbors would respond and told the kids to wash it off, quick.

Farrow & Ball had to photoshop lattice over the three-foot stoop because I forgot that the guys who came to repair it never finished the job. An older hydrangea bush and poison ivy crawled up from underneath. Later that summer, the lattice still not on, I dressed in a long shirt, long pants, plastic garden gloves, and a cloth mask, and as my children watched, I yanked the poison ivy from the roots with a closed fist, recalling fist fighting my peers when they made comments about my lack of Blackness on my vitiligo-speckled body. Close your eyes. Yank. Pull. Throw it in the bag. The little girl in me did not leave. Neither did the Brooklyn in me on our excursion up.

"The color black is a noncolor," River explained to me on the walk down DeKalb in Brooklyn, a few months later, after dinner one night. "If you move the color gradient from orange on, then you *kind of* get black. And same is true for brown. They aren't real colors!"

"That sounds a lot like colorism to me!" I said, to which Oak chimed in, "It's not colorism, because there's no color!" Adobe, for what it's worth, agrees with my children. According to their scientific and artistic view, "Black isn't on the visible spectrum of color. All other colors are reflections of light, except black. Black is the absence of light. Unlike white and other hues, pure black can exist in nature without any light at all."

The visibility (invisibility) of our Blackness didn't just extend itself to the street and the new home we were creating, it seeped into the colors I chose to use in the house and the tools that I decided to use to restore it. The stories of Blackness and Black womanhood, and how we fix not only things within our homes but also our children and society, are often up for interpretation and translation by us and those who we allow in our window.

In 1843, Emily Warren Roebling, a white woman, was born to an upper-middle-class family in Cold Spring, New York, the second-youngest of twelve children. In 1865, she married Washington Roebling (a white man) after exchanging letters for eleven months. Washington's father, John A. Roebling, a German-born American civil engineer (also a white man), had invented the twisted wire cables that made the suspension of bridges like the Brooklyn Bridge possible. He died from decompression sickness, and soon after, his son Washington Roebling fell ill with the same sickness, from working beneath the bend in a caisson as he built the bridge's piers. Emily, worried that her husband would suffer the same fate as his father, began ferociously writing notes, dictating next steps to workers, learning materials, analyzing plans. She became such a prominent figure in the building of the Brooklyn Bridge that many believed that she was the original mastermind behind the project to begin with. When the bridge was done, Emily rode along it with President Chester Arthur, who praised her effort. Names like Emily Warren Roebling's were eagerly taught to my daughter on a field trip as we crossed under the Brooklyn Bridge, our brown backs facing the Hudson while we looked up. The teachers pointed out nuts and bolts that Emily directed, but I wondered all the while: Who did the physical labor? It is extremely difficult to find any information on the freed African American folks who may have made the dream of that bridge a reality.

President Arthur's history as New York City activist and lawyer prior to the building of the bridge suggests that freed Blacks worked on it. In his most prominent case, the 1860 Lemmon slave case, the New York Supreme Court ruled that enslaved people being transferred to a slave state through New York would be freed. Arthur, an early organizer, joined the Republican Party, which was established by anti-slavery activists in 1854. Prior to that, only two months after passing the bar, he used those organizing skills to successfully represent Elizabeth Jennings Graham, a twenty-seven-year-old schoolteacher who boarded and refused to leave a segregated New York City streetcar that declined service to African Americans. Graham's mother, Elizabeth Cartwright Jennings, was a founding member of Ladies Literary Society of New York, an organization composed of New York's elite Black women, who created community in reading, raising money for enslaved folks, and, of course, writing as a means of self-improvement. Her daughter didn't stray too far from under her mother's wing and used writing her account of the events and the distribution of the story to papers like *The North Star* and the *New-York Daily Tribune* to call national attention to the segregation of the rail lines, and the effects on the Black community. "I told him, I was a respectable person, born and raised in New York, did not know where he was born and that he was a good-for-nothing impudent fellow for insulting decent persons while on their way to church," Jennings wrote. Elizabeth Jennings Graham won her case, eventually leading to the desegregation of all New York transit lines—her use of writing as a critical tool of activism powerfully shaped her position as the "nineteenth-century Rosa Parks."

Although the power of Jennings's words endured, the peace found was short-lived. Ten years later: the draft riots, a result of the conscription of all male citizens between the ages of twenty and thirty-five, and unmarried men between the ages of thirty-five and forty-five, subjected men to military duty and cities to mayhem. This mandate most deeply affected working-class and poor white Irish men, as the buyout of service was well over a year's salary at the time. Black people became the target of violence, as they were free from this obligation since they were not yet considered citizens. Not yet considered human. Not yet considered fully free. *Black is a noncolor.* The anger pulsated through New York, Boston, and even Detroit—white mobs destroying neighborhoods and bloodying streets in their wake.

For months, the tiny red toolbox in the Mae House shifted its position on the six-seater wood dining room table where the espresso dining chairs found their place. Its contents: food-safe wood wax, half-inch finishing nails, epoxy filler, caulk, sealant, three different-size paint scrapers, a wire brush, and some found items. The box was disordered, but that was easily overlooked considering the table where it perched was a mess of names of anonymous teenagers, carved in with

X-ACTO knives—first true loves inside oversize hearts, and an anarchist sign on the left side. The table arrived from Detroit, Michigan, on a pallet heavier than the table itself. Steel rope and bolted legs, soggy country grass, and a high stoop made it impossible for me to bring the table in by myself. It remained out front while I called my assistant, my then boyfriend, and another friend, fighting through the fear that I had taken on too much. It was part of a bigger admission: I was financially and in many ways, functionally, single—doing this alone, indefinitely.

Eventually, I texted my realtor, who reminded me to call Gerry, the "can do anything" man from Brooklyn who now lived upstate full-time, but with an accent thick enough to prove his origins. He was unusually reliable, but only to a point—fixing the molded steps to satisfy the bank for closing in May, but never painting them; knocking down my kitchen cabinets within an hour in June, but never sending an invoice; using a metal lift to place the cast-iron soaking tub in the back of a pickup truck, with a kid waving out the truck's front window. "I'll be over in an hour," he said about the table. Gerry arrived in a bright green T-shirt, whipped a silver-covered box cutter out from his back pocket, and ordered two gentlemen to grab the edges of the table and wobble it in inch by inch. They placed it in the living room. One of the guys ignorantly pointed to the anarchist sign, calling it a swastika. Afraid my purchase might offend Gerry, I began to sweat and apologize. I shared the story about how the table came from an art school in Detroit, salvaged by a Black woman. Gerry seemed intrigued and unbothered.

When they left, I shimmied the table to the dining room with beads of sweat rolling past my top lip, elated and relieved that it was inside. I sent my assistant a photo, then my boyfriend, and sat at the head of it. I traced the gray etchings with my index finger and typed to myself, "I can't always fix it, but I can surely hire someone else who can. That's my power." I posted a photo of the table on

Instagram, the company I purchased it from, Woodward Throwbacks, reposting with, "So happy it's there."

I longed to speak to someone—a woman, a Black woman—who *could* fix things with their hands so easily. How did she do it? Was it natural? A skill born out of desire or need? I sat there with the sliding door open, a family of wasps hovering around the outdoor sconce, swirling through the wrought iron double S-hook I drilled next to it a week prior in anticipation of fall string lights. Bo Shepherd came to mind. Bo is half of the Woodward Throwbacks team that salvaged the dining room table and restored it with new screws and better legs. They offered to sand and finish it for me, but I declined, opting for the full story instead.

Elizabeth Jennings Graham escaped the city with her husband, mother, and sister for New Jersey. According to the late John H. Hewitt's research of Graham, published in 1990, shortly before their move, Elizabeth and her husband suffered the tragic loss of their young son. They buried him in the moist soil of Cypress Hill Cemetery in Brooklyn, the same cemetery where my grandmother, great-grandmother, great-uncle, and many other kinfolk are laid to rest.

It would take calm to be restored in the city after the end of the rioting, and the death of her husband, for Elizabeth to return home to New York. She used her homecoming as an opportunity to open the first kindergarten for Black children in New York City, located at 247 West Forty-first Street, where she also lived. She worked at the school until she passed away in 1901. During the summer of 2022, I considered Elizabeth's life often, along with a quote from W.E.B. Du Bois: "Children learn more from what you are than what you teach." Had the children in that first class and the ones thereafter known of her act of bravery on that streetcar, her refusal to give up her seat? Were they aware of the court case that came after? Had they become accustomed to the legacy of her resistance they were in fact living? Was that hard-won freedom obvious to those students in the restored Harlem where they lived? Could they feel it in their bodies, inside Jennings's home, in that ground-floor Black school, the first of its kind when it opened?

By December of 2021, the copper pipes in the primary bathroom of the Mae House had yet to be rerouted. The bathroom had been gutted since October. Another surge of Covid sat on top of the city. My ex-boyfriend returned to Europe after spending three weeks in New York with us. My brain was already foggy from the financial and physical tasks of the renovation. I shuffled back and forth between upstate and the city for single days and overnights to manage workers. I blindly transferred thousands of dollars without contracts and learned to communicate in many languages to get through to the men. I leaned on my ex-boyfriend the most during his three-week visit that fall to help me manage the kids while I managed the renovation. He picked up where he could, how he always had.

During his stay, A, my nanny of four years, gave me notice of his departure, and I collapsed on the couch as if someone had died. "You don't understand, he is the only way I can do all of this!" I cried. "Who is going to feed them when I can't? Or pick them up from school? Fold the laundry when I'm on a shoot? Or fix the doorknob?" In response, my ex grew silent and almost reluctantly put his right hand on my left leg to comfort me. The next day in the kitchen, I got angry at A when he called to clarify his departure, and in response, my ex got angry at me.

"We can ease out of this," A said. "I'd like to take the other full-time job by the end of the year, and that would give you and the kids some time to adjust."

"We need to move, and I have to finish this book," I responded. "Is it okay to wait until January?" He said that of course it was okay. He didn't want to leave us high and dry. "You've really helped me during this time—and I want to keep helping you all, too." A's reassurances worked like a balm, and I let my shoulders fall over our curry-stained Formica counters. As it turned out, though, A would not stay on until January. He hardly stayed on through December. One Covid scare in his family, then another, a handful of mismatched work dates with his blooming full-time job, and one day, he was no longer part of our unit, shuffling around our home with us.

In December, the air shifted in New York. The sun did not shine. The new pipe colors for the Mae House primary bathroom were chosen like tile samples: red and blue—one for cold and one for hot. For the first time in five years, the heat hardly turned on, and my Brooklyn apartment turned bitterly cold some days and evenings. To combat it, we danced to Otis Redding, layered wool and cotton blankets, and relished the meager warmth that did bother to thump from the radiator. We planned Christmas with the belief that little gifts were acceptable considering our impending move, and we placed things we no longer needed on our brick stoop. When Omicron continued to rise, we canceled the return of our annual holiday party and opted to move it to February instead. The house renovation stalled as every contractor fell ill, and with my nanny and then boyfriend both out of our lives, I craved ways to fill the yawning hole that comes with losing your foundation.

"Why don't we meet Ti Ti for Christmas Eve dinner?" I proposed to River and Oak.

"Yes!" they screamed in unison as we sorted their baby toys from their big-kid toys one afternoon. That night, we headed to meet my sister out for dinner, in search of a little warmth and good cheer.

My landlord's lawyers changed a few times that year, and we were unable to reach a settlement. In response, I held on to our apartment, my rent, the moratorium that held New York State and its residents' welfare together, and also a bit of hope. That evening around midnight, with the building hallway pitch-black, my landlord banged on my door, looking for me. "LaTonya, next time you need to call the cops," my lawyer wrote in the wee hours the next morning. But calling the cops felt like a non-option. I had the cops called on me once by my ex, who had relapsed again. Five months prior, Philando Castile was shot dead in Falcon Heights, a suburb of St. Paul, Minnesota, when picking up his girlfriend, Diamond Reynolds, and their four-year-old daughter from their apartment. Back then, River was five. Oak was two. When I refused to let my ex in our home that night on Christmas Eve, an argument between us ensued. He had been struggling with sobriety for a while and was clearly intoxicated. Afraid he'd wake the children, I let him in and begged him not to drink inside. I grabbed his bottles and began pouring them down our kitchen sink, the gold knob of our light green cabinets knocking at my left hip. He grabbed my right hand, wrestling my body away from his six-pack, and I slapped him away in defense, demanding that he release me. Instantly, he dropped the glass bottles in the sink and let me go. And then he called the police.

I knew what cops did to Black women. It did not take Breonna Taylor's killing in Louisville to teach me. I knew what happened to kids whose parents fought at home. The childhood memory of my mother being handcuffed in the mid-'90s in Silver Spring, Maryland, and escorted out of our townhouse apartment on Valentine's Day taught me that.

That Christmas Eve, I stood with my hands at my sides when the four officers arrived, a colorful collection of characters, including one Black woman, I noted. I thought about it being the holidays, their mercy, my clean house, my still-sleeping babies in their beds. My ex blabbered on in the dusty checkered-floored hallway while I robotically escorted them through our sublevel apartment, nervously appeasing to their good. "Please, my children are sleeping. Please," I begged. I told them that I asked him not to call. That I never wanted him to show up like this. "I'm a good mother," I said. "Look how clean it is in here. Tomorrow is Christmas. I'm scared. Please." The officer shut the door to the kids' room and walked me to the living room, hands still at my sides, unwilling to move an inch in their gaze in my home. "You need to leave him. He could get you arrested, and your kids could be taken away from you," one of the officers whispered to me. In the hallway, another officer pestered my ex about his intentions and said much of the same. They requested he leave, return the next day when he sobered up, and said they'd follow up in two days to check in. "Next time, you'll both be arrested," they said sternly to him as they exited the building. On Christmas morning, I opened gifts with my children alone on our floor, traumatized and relieved. *We don't call the cops to our homes,* I thought when I read my lawyer's email on a different Christmas Eve, as I dressed my children for burgers and fries.

The day after, on my kick to reclaim what family foundation looked like, the kids and I rode the Q train from DeKalb Avenue to Canal Street, where red-and-green string lights stretched from sidewalk edge to sidewalk edge, and a surprising number of tourists funneled out of the train station with us. We weaved through crowds onto Broadway in our holiday best and neon N95 masks, hoping to dodge the ghost of Christmas present. After a few minutes of failed turns, we found what we were looking for: a little shop set between Chinatown and Little Italy, with a tiny side door and bell, a wraparound counter with crystals of various purposes and sizes, and a corner chair tucked behind an armoire. "We're here!" Oak shouted as I buzzed the bell, our cold hands waving through the glass door. We had our auras read, a kaleidoscope of colors pasted to a matte-black frame, hoping to reveal something about who we were and what we'd become.

"You have a hard time with your words. You have to try and speak all the things you have to say," the reader said to Oak. "*Oh, your heart,*" she added after a few more beats. I glanced at him, preparing my speech about how a few years before, he'd spent four days on Thirty-first Street at NYU Langone for his open-heart surgery. I'd put photos on his side table and brought his favorite stuffed animals to make the best of our temporary hospital home as his tiny body was broken open to repair what he was born with—a ventricular septal defect. A wound and a mend to save a future self that only I could imagine as his mother.

When it was my turn, I stood in front of the reader, chest out, nervous about what she may see in the arch of pink and orange that illuminated from my 'fro. "You love so much," she said through her mask. I gently, slightly pulled down mine, as if it would allow me to hear her better. "You care a lot about community and talking and love. So much love."

The next day, on Christmas morning, Oak awoke with a cough, a tickle that became persistent throughout the day. Over the course of the morning, the cough turned into a runny nose, and I knew the source. When we were done opening our gifts, my sister called to say that she took a Covid test, and it was positive—a swift change from the day before we met when she took a mandatory one for work, which was negative. The memory of the next few days is foggy, only pieced together in my head through film photographs I shot over the course of the nearly three weeks isolated in my apartment with my children. I found the film eight months later when we were decluttering for our move, scans of Oak and River, lying on the sofa in a makeshift sickbed. Our blue couch pillows surrounding their bodies like rafts. Dry snacks of bananas and crackers in the middle, drinks on the hardwood floor, the cats, Langston and St. James, flanking each side. Later, Oak zooming through the frame, only visible by his head of curls. River, limp on the sofa, visibly weak, a tie-dye mask around her mouth, her legs crisscrossed. Covid hit her the hardest, despite both of their double vaccinations. It was relentless, more than flu-like. There are photos of me, too, that Oak snapped between it all; often in the kitchen, a brown clay mug at the small marble bistro table, a mask on and off, sturdy, half smiling. I remember how tired I was, how exhausted from realizing that, despite the handful of friends that brought medicine and groceries to my door, we were all dependent on me and only me. My childhood diagnosis of lupus possessed me. If I were to get sick—really sick, I presumed—I wasn't quite sure how my children would fare without me at the helm. So I stayed away as much as I could, I took care of them from a distance, and I snapped photos, unable to let go of documenting the way it may happen. Eventually, I tucked my body in my squeaky queen-size bed between my children, singing hallucinatory lullabies about how mammals sleep with their young.

In a collection of theoretical essays for her 1989 book, *Talking Back: Thinking Feminist, Thinking Black*, bell hooks writes:

> There are some folks for whom openness is not about the luxury of "will I choose to share this or tell that," but rather, "will I survive—will I make it through—will I stay alive." And openness is about how to be well and telling the truth is about how to put the broken bits and pieces of the heart back together again. It is about being whole, being wholehearted.

Will I survive this? was a recurring question that winter, but it showed up in three prominent ways: Once when the kids had Covid. Another time when my heart broke for the third time with my ex-boyfriend. The second happened in between these two events, shortly after the kids recovered from their illnesses. The kids and I rang in the new year, finally recuperated, me having slipped Covid's grasp entirely. The relief and elation kept me buzzing around our apartment; strewing New Year's Eve paper chains along the dining room walls, picking out our fanciest outfits, blowing up oversize gold confetti balloons to hang in the living room. We had cake their dad made and sent over, blasted music, and had what we called a *fancy* dance party! I wore velvet and imagined all of us at some underground speakeasy—both of them in their twenties, me in my forties, laughing at their childhood years spent indoors.

When we danced too much and the breath was knocked out of River, we collapsed in a fit of laughter on our couch. I kept snapping photos, even when the heat refused to turn on. One evening, after the kids had fallen asleep in my bed, I dug through the blue tin with brown gingerbread houses that I kept in the built-in closet key area. The tin was full of metal things, a collection of bits and bobs I kept instead of trying my hand at the oversize bin of metal scraps and tools the kids' dad left at our apartment six years ago and never took with him. Or the nineteen-inch plastic, orange contractor's toolbox that stored the more practical larger tools he left—and I added to—over the years. The tin reminded me of the tins of chunky peeling crayons my grandmother kept around for us to play with in her Brooklyn apartment in the '90s, left over from her earlier days of being a substitute teacher at PS 316. Similarly, the kids had one, too, upstate at the house. There were no crayons in this tin, but like the act of coloring, I could use it to try to reorient the way I saw something.

That evening, I googled "how to drain a radiator." To my surprise, the search resulted in clear, concise directions, but warned against doing it yourself. Our apartment was too cold, though. And I spent a good portion of the last few months building up my own stamina with projects at the Mae House, enough to believe that I could do this task safely. I began knocking on the radiators, using a small silver Husky wrench, then oscillated between two different sizes in the mini wrench set. A white tattered cotton rag and a green pot accompanied me. First, the radiator in the dining room, which I had heard the handyman say two years ago was "directly over the boiler." Then, the radiator to the right in the living room. *A little warm. Warmer. Okay, better*, I thought as the steam released. You're not supposed to bleed a radiator without a key, but I was capable and handy. We were cold, I repeated again and again. Then the radiator to the left of the living room, under the window, beside our fiddle leaf tree that shed seven well leaves that winter. The screw was tight, the wrench barely making a dent, save for chipping off a dime-size piece of the ten-year-old gold spray paint my friend put on them for décor purposes in the gray painted room. When the screw loosened a little more, no steam or even water released. So I went farther, ever slightly, hoping to catch the tiniest drips. *Whoosh!* A geyser of black warm soot began to expel out of the radiator. It shot straight on the walls, dumped itself on the carpet, soaked the curtains, plummeted on the leaves, turning them nearly brown within minutes.

I held the spot where the water released with my left hand, like holding a person's gunshot-wounded leg, attempting to minimize the blood loss in the massacre. I called for River, who, sleepy and confused, found me breathing heavy, sopping with black water. "Hold this while I look for the screw!" I demanded. She became my ER nurse; I became the doctor. I swam through the water on our hardwood floors, no screw or even tiny metal wrench revealing itself. I grabbed two towels. "Mommy, it's everywhere!" River said in a cracking voice. I lifted the living room window and ordered River to find my phone to call her father. She couldn't find my phone, and soon enough, Oak awoke, crying, nervously asking, "Mommy, what can I do?"

"Grab towels!" I directed, my own tears breaking through my stone face, assuming somehow we were all going to drown together in this sea of black water, in this apartment of all my fears, misgivings, and mess. I screamed out the window, "Someone help us, pleasseeeeeee!" I heard folks giggling in the distance, my own yells falling deaf on our busy block. "*Help, please!*" River stood there, swishing the towels around as the black water consumed our white carpet even more and the cats took cover in another room. "River, go ring Casey's bell!" I instructed. Casey was our neighbor, another mom, a reliable friend, a source when everything would go to shit. Either River didn't ring or they were asleep, but River returned, saying she couldn't figure it out. Soon she found her iPad and used that to call her dad. "*Come!*" she yelled. He started to ask questions. "*Don't ask, Daddy, just come!"* The water began to subside, retreating to its anonymous ocean, and as it did, River found the screw tucked under the radiator.

Their dad arrived as I finally sat, after River switched into clean clothes and Oak returned to bed. I cried, breathless, chattering words and broken sentences, knowing I looked insane, but unable to compose myself in the aftermath. "Mommy, it's all okay now," River said through tears, patting my back. I had never wanted my daughter to be the kind of daughter that I had to be, one that had to take care of her mother in despair. But there she was, mothering me. "It's okay now, Mommy. It's all okay now. We are fine."

"I'm so sorry, River," I kept repeating. River returned to my bed, bidding good night to her father, my tears still rolling. "Have you been drinking?" he asked. My crying stopped immediately. Slowly, I made my way back to myself, realizing then that the bubble of safety that enveloped my home had been briefly penetrated. "It's time for you to go," I responded. I hadn't had anything to drink in two months.

The heat from the radiators never really came on that winter. My efforts to call 311 were hardly answered. And when they weren't, I used portable heaters in between it all to heat our home. On January 9, 2022, a fire broke out at a residential building in the Bronx due to a defective space heater, rattling the largely West African residents. The fire killed seventeen people, including eight children. To blame? Faulty electrical wiring and the inoperable nature of self-closing doors that were supposed to prevent such a catastrophe. The next day, I ripped a piece of paper out of Oak's drawing book and pulled a permanent marker from our junk drawer, throwing the heater in the trash with a note: "KILLS PEOPLE."

With all of the gutting of the Mae House finished, the renovation ramped up in earnest that winter. I lovingly started to call it a *restoration*, as the pieces of the old house were put back and the new parts that I dreamed up replaced what was broken. During my weekends at the house to document and assess the process, I spent time at Al-Anon meetings to help cope with my ex's issues. I logged on to videoconferences with hundreds of others, quietly sobbing with my camera off whenever the words cut close to the bone. As the house finished, my practice with Al-Anon evolved into daily, sometimes twice-a-day meditation, staring at the tiny red toolbox on the table, from the kids' den—now the meditation room—willing for things to be completed soon enough. Then, I would move the toolbox, move my body, and likewise, my fog would move. "This is just a season," a girlfriend reminded me as we rotated paint cans, painted cabinets, cleaned cobwebs, purchased plants, and watched as I replaced knobs on the kitchen cabinet doors with mismatched curated ones with my very own drill, pressing holes, filling them, twisting in, moving on. I was tired, mentally, physically, and only buoyed by the net placed under me by my girlfriends.

We finished the largest renovations of the Mae House after three weeks of scrambling for the Farrow & Ball shoot. I had put them off for far too long, and spring was thawing out winter's edge. The red toolbox was the last thing to be put away early that morning before they arrived, messily stuffed, and placed on a shelf in the basement away from the camera's eye. It hadn't occurred to me that the house was a healer, a distractor, a liberator during the winter where I watched walls open and close again, pipes rerouted, tubs installed, fixtures placed. I yearned to call my ex-boyfriend throughout all of those scenarios (even, and especially, the gruesome ones), wanting to feel as if I weren't physically alone taking on this lifetime of work. But I knew each and every time that restoration was mine to do. With the house nearly finished, there alone in the living room on the green couch, I listened attentively to Mahalia Jackson:

> *Precious Lord, take my hand*
> *Lead me on, let me sta-and*

"How do you feel now that the house is finished?" the producer for the Farrow & Ball shoot asked while I stood in the kitchen next to the light switch I painted twice the evening before, trying to match the shade perfectly in the daylight. "Well, it's all just beginning. And it doesn't ever really feel done, I don't think. The work is never really done."

Two months later, there were rumors of *Roe v. Wade* being overturned. A few days after that, ten Black elders were shot in a Tops grocery store. It was live streamed. What seemed like a reconnection with my ex-boyfriend during the production of Farrow & Ball fizzled into poor communication and chaos. It wasn't my ex's fault entirely. To his credit, I spent the last four years exponentially growing and healing wounds with him by my side, and he, healing with me by his. But that particular scar was deepened because of him and all the men before him: my ex-husband, my father, the ones who touched me without consent, the sheriffs who evicted my family when I was a kid, and all the other men who shaped home for me, for good. Even the ones I reluctantly let renovate the Mae House, when I wanted women who knew how to fix and what not to from the very start—from that first meeting with Katherine, and her afternoon in the garden, and evening with the architect, and all the women I dreamed of hiring to sow into the house. Women, specifically Black women, know all too well the road of reparations. In her 2021 book, *On Freedom: Four Songs of Care and Constraint*, Maggie Nelson highlights the ecology of the past as a punitive, paranoid, and "reparative reading" practice that so many of us want, need, and do take, as first argued by queer theorist Eve Sedgwick. Nelson writes of Sedgwick's work:

> Her description of reparative practice as a means of "assembl[ing] and confer[ring] plentitude on an object that will then have resources to offer to an inchoate self" makes audible its potential relationship to art: by attending to the "richest reparative practices"

of others and ourselves, Sedgwick argued, we can learn more about "the many ways selves and communities succeed in extracting suspense from the objects of a culture . . . whose avowed desire has often been not to sustain them." What's more, reparative practices are alive with paradox, and decidedly *not* always performed by solicitous people overflowing with a healing "regard for others."

My curated relationship with the Mae House came from a deep practice of not necessarily wanting to repair whatever harm may have been done to people by offering them rest but to provide folks with "a utopian blueprint for a possible future," as described by academic José Esteban Muñoz. If I share, may it not only repair but sustain.

In tandem with the house, I dove deep into my own body's restoration that spring. I meditated more with my hand on my heart in the house, at my apartment, down the street, in the garden, with my kids in the deep green high grass, repeating these words from Swami Kripalu, Bapuji:

> My beloved child, break your heart no longer
>
> [. . .]
> Let no one, No thing or ideal or ideas obstruct you
> If one comes, even in the name of "Truth,"
> Forgive it for its unknowing
> Do not fight.
> Let go
>
> And breathe into the goodness that you are.

And when there were pauses, I etched an Al-Anon phrase in pencil and taped it to my phone and in my head: "I didn't cause it, I can't control it, and I certainly can't fix it." I considered my connection to New York City between these moments and found hidden messaging in the walls while stepping back to stare at everything I managed to pull together during that time. Maybe the Mae House's job cut the cord to the storyline I had always told myself about my body, my home within myself. Perhaps it rearranged my physical sense of home, too.

James Baldwin's escape from the United States has always fascinated me. In the summer of 2022, I proclaimed I could no longer stand the city, this failing nation, and booked my children and me tickets to Europe for July, when the fog from my season of grief started to lift. We brought three carry-ons, and when I went to think about what to pack, the only tools I knew I needed were my children, the meetings, the knowledge the house was doing its work, and the meditation.

We kept with our routine in Paris and in Berlin for three weeks. I drank Americanos on nonexistent Berlin stoops. We mapped our way through the city with my ever-dying phone—walking down Kottbusser Damm, riding bikes on Maybachufer. We weeded through crowds of other brown folks on Sonnen-allee, stopping to ask for water at corner stores while I stuck AirPods in my ears, listening to three hundred other strangers anonymously share about grief and restoration in those Al-Anon meetings. My children had no idea about the emotional weight I was attempting to lighten for them and me. Between, we flew to Paris as the clock struck midnight on my thirty-third birthday, shopped at Merci with avocados and baguettes in our bags, rode the rides at the fair in Jardin des Tuileries, and scoured our Airbnb's plastic toolbox for phone chargers that worked.

Crabs molt from April until fall, their new selves no longer fitting into old homes. They detach, cracks along their shell, thinning from within with the help of the water. To preserve energy, they hold very tiny components of their old shell for their future home. Until it forms (a phenomenon that can reverse if not the right place or time), the crab remains soft, vulnerable. Our Europe trip was the first time River and Oak left the country, and it was my second time in Paris. Back in Berlin, I thought of Audre Lorde and Berlin being this bridge in her life during her breast cancer diagnosis, a space of healing between America and St. Croix, where she also spent much of her time. Buoying myself with these thoughts, I let my body and those of my children float in the warmth of the Schlachtensee, like babies comforted in the amniotic sac. Convinced that the problem was America and New York City's post-pandemic oppressiveness, I applied to an English-speaking private school for the kids, argued successfully with my ex-husband for the opportunity to leave temporarily, and found an apartment with an oversize kitchen island and a wooden bunk bed custom-made for another eleven-year-old and eight-year-old in Neukölln. I just needed time away, this time. A future time. Time to rest. Time to heal. Time to restore.

Back in New York, the Mae House's renovation process finished. Its doors opened, creating a safe space for its first Black families at sliding-scale rates and no cost. They picked tomatoes out of the raised beds, stir-fried kale on the grill, and made their own bouquets out of marigolds and cosmos. It secured a coveted spot on *Domino* magazine's summer issue, "Rest Assured," and the video I shot with Farrow & Ball finally went live on their social media channels. In the video, I stand in the kitchen that I designed and painted with girlfriends, with the pain mostly out of sight in my eyes, and my hair in cornrows. I cut all my hair off before our trip to Europe—"Part of my cycle," I claimed—and when back in New York, like the Mae House, I started to feel that I was becoming more myself, shorter hair and all. Or rather, I was coming into whatever new self stood on the other side of it all.

Anyone who has ever renovated anything knows that renovations don't always turn out exactly how we plan. Back from Europe, we never heard from the international school, despite the paperwork and intense follow-up for weeks. I sent River and Oak to their public schools by September 9, 2022, and gave the

Berlin apartment notice that we wouldn't make it by the fifteenth. The anniversary of my father's death rolled around later that week, and for the first time ever, I didn't feel alienated by the lack of his physical presence, as I had when he was alive, or by the sheer disappearance of him in his death. Abandonment, possibly temporarily, didn't haunt me like some ghost in my mental attic anymore.

Feeling a return to my own body, I had sex with a Black man for the first time. It's hard—and a bit mortifying—to admit, but I was a seventeen-year-old virgin when I had my first and only Black boyfriend. Now, years later, I watched this man's body shadow mine as I shadowed his, both of us delineating the pain of our losses on each other. As his beaded drops of sweat fell on my tabletop-flat chest, with my eyes briefly closed, I had visions of the undrinkable water flowing out of the faucets of the 150,000 predominantly Black residents in Jackson, Mississippi, who had been without clean water for eight weeks. When I peeled my eyes open to stare into his, I gasped at the audacity of reparations, of healing, of the liberating practice of being with him, in this home of homes, in this country, where so much of what we do is not deemed safe.

The weekend before the fall equinox, I received a certified letter. Despite our attempts at negotiations to mediate, I was being brought to court for a holdover case to be evicted from our apartment. This case was brought on in May—if I moved prior to Berlin, I would have missed the date entirely. In need of the relief of the soaking tub, I took the train up to the Mae House again, this time after it hosted a trans-residency group's founders for a few days, who posited the question, "Care over impact?" and left me a pin on the couch side table that read, "God Keeps His Promises." That weekend, I made bouquets of black-eyed Susans, *Rudbeckia hirta*, native to the land on which the Mae House sits, an ancient symbol of encouragement and justice. It is said to be a pioneer plant, because it often blooms despite natural disasters, where very little has survived.

I went down to the basement and removed the little red toolbox, placing it on its first home, the wood table, organizing its contents bit by bit, until it looked useful and peaceful to the eye. Until it became a place where I could easily return. On the way back home to New York City the next morning, I scrolled through new apartments on my phone, saying prayers for our specific needs, the pin the guests left clipped to my chest, while I watched the sun dip low behind the Hudson River, illuminating the sky in a cast of orange. Between Poughkeepsie and Croton-Harmon, I read a piece of Toni Morrison's novel *Home:*

> The final set of Cee's healing had been, for her, the worst. She was to be sun-smacked, which meant spending at least one hour a day with her legs spread open to the blazing sun. Each woman agreed that that embrace would rid her of any remaining womb sickness.

A few days later, I texted the guy I had slept with a little bit of the story of the Mae House and a note about my body. He wrote back, "I'm glad you're home."

Wayward

The child in each of us
Knows paradise.
Paradise is home.
Home as it was
Or home as it should have been.

Paradise is one's own place,
One's own people,
One's own world,
Knowing and known,
Perhaps even
Loving and loved.

—OCTAVIA E. BUTLER

n December 2020, as I folded stacks of children's clothes on my living room floor, leaning up against the nonworking fireplace (the warmest place in the house on a cold winter's day), I listened to a previously recorded episode of *On Being* between Krista Tippett and Mary Catherine Bateson, a writer and cultural anthropologist. Krista asks Mary Catherine about the linguistics of composing life, and as she reads one of Bateson's quotes, you can hear the fascination in her voice.

"I like to think of men and women as artists of their own lives, working with what comes to hand through accident or talent to compose and recompose a pattern in time that expresses who they are and what they believe in, making meaning even as they are studying and working and raising children, creating and re-creating themselves," read Tippett in a clear and calming voice.

I stop folding and hit the plus sign on the Sonos speaker. Krista asks Mary Catherine what the word *homemaking* holds for her. And Bateson responds with prose that I've kept written on a sticky note taped at each corner on the wall in the entryway of my apartment since:

> Well, creating an environment in which learning is possible. And that is what a home is. I mean that is what we want the homes that we give to our children to be—places where they grow in many, many different ways. They learn how to connect with other people. They learn how to care for others. They learn particular skills. They learn their own capacities and how to trust other people and how to trust themselves. They learn what respect is.

"On January 2nd 2021, Mary Catherine passed away at the age of 81, still writing her newest book, *Love Across Difference*, about how diversity of all stripes—gender, culture, and nationality—can be a source of insight, collaboration, and creativity," says *The New York Times.* Her legacy as a cultural anthropologist taught women that life was an improvisatory art.

The first church my mother created, a Church with No Walls, was its own work of art. She built it the year I had River, and this newly formed woman had a relationship with God before her relationship with me. The powers of my mother transferred, and church members became her family. She knew church could be had anywhere—most especially in the bottom floor of her brownstone apartment. This church and its members, who included young women, older friends, and folks like me, whose relationship to God was ever waning and growing, held a belief so great, it didn't need the typical structure to define it. This fascinates me now, creating space beyond the physical spaces we thought we relied on. They had church, and we make home, ultimately, without walls.

It is a hard task, and building and rearranging is now even more daunting than it felt years prior. My children grab masks from key hanger hooks and strap them across their faces to protect those who enter, to protect themselves. On walks, we watch a man ride a bicycle on the wrong side of Broadway under tenement buildings with new construction façades under signs that read, "Finally, Back Together." The kids read the sign aloud as we walk back home, where the mess waits, but it is ours.

I am not entirely sure of what will come of the Mae House, of us, and of you, too. But I repeat these things like evening prayers:

> We are to shield, and we are to learn.
> We are to create, and we are to undo.
> The terrifying is connected to the joy.
> The inside of our homes is shaped by the outside.
> A *living* home is always porous.

Epilogue

In contrast, gift economies arise from the abundance of gifts from the Earth, which are owned by no one and therefore shared. Sharing engenders relationships of goodwill and bonds that ensure you will be invited to the feast when your neighbor is fortunate. Security is ensured by nurturing the bonds of reciprocity.

—*Robin Wall Kimmerer*

It was April 2023 when we celebrated a year of the Mae House in operation. Three serving bowls, several mismatched plates from Brooklyn, and others that remained at the house were arranged on top of two long folding tables pressed against each other—twelve wooden and metal chairs tucked underneath. A ripped duvet cover that once belonged to River, dyed with roses and hibiscus, served as a tablecloth, along with another made from leftover archival textiles from ace&jig. Behind the table, golden forsythia began its bloom, which would go on for nearly three more weeks before the flowers began to turn green, making way for goldenrod, echinacea, and aster. The food was overflowing: rice, avocado, *tamalitos veganos, sopa de platano, curtido de jicama,* and salsa lovingly made by the mother of a mutual friend. Bottles of orange wine filled in the empty spots on the table, as did mandarins brought in by the handfuls from friends. It seemed as if rain would be in the forecast, but we had planned the day too much to reschedule it, or even easier, move the event indoors. And so we set up with the hopes

that the guests would come and the sun would shine. Fortunately, both did. Every seat at the table was filled, and the sun made an appearance just as I stood up to read portions of "The Serviceberry," an essay of Robin Wall Kimmerer's that was published the October prior. We had survived that year by tooth and nail, goodwill, and truly, nearly a broken spirit or two from me.

Whenever people asked about how everything at the house was going, my response always was (and is), "It's doing what it needs to do in the world." Although there are times when I'm unsure about what this looks like exactly, I continue to return to the house as a point of reorientation, to remind me of what I have done and where I am going.

The deed of the Mae House is mine alone. It was mine to birth. It is mine to keep alive, to pay for, and to develop. But just as my children are mine but also belong to the world—and I ask others to help rear them for an earth that seems to rapidly change and decrease within moments—the same is true for the house. It is for me, and for others, to nurture. Statistically, 95 percent of our regular-rate rentals within our first year were from BIPOC, a shockingly high figure that illuminated much of the work I wrote to you in these pages. We care and gift to one another in a way that often mimics the way the land and the plants do for us. In a way that we have known for generations.

As we gathered at the house that afternoon for our one-year anniversary, the shift in my spirit was palpable. The availability of not just the house but of myself to the world was tangible. Although I hadn't quite known what exactly, something else was nearing its own state of aliveness.

Cleaning the house after the celebration and getting ready to head back to the city, I noticed the red toolbox that remained where it was the year prior—no longer beckoning me to undertake yet another new project. I passed it on my way down to the basement to collect three gallons of paint that remained, and stacked them in a silver granny cart for the train ride home. Green for one of the kids' rooms in our new apartment, one blue for Nicole, who helps manage the house rentals and is a dear friend, and Middleton pink for our living room/dining room in Brooklyn. Middleton pink is known for its ability to change in the light, and our living room is sandwiched between both the kids' rooms and two filtered privacy windows. Light is sparse, but it does come in. Always, no matter what we may endure.

The week after the celebration, the kids were on spring break, and on the first day I woke them up by singing "Optimistic" by Sounds of Blackness (as I frequently do), with paintbrushes in hand. Drop cloths lay over our floor, a few boxes were stacked in corners, and the cats, however big they are now, hid under our new raised countertops.

"River, after you eat, you'll do that wall. Oak, you'll do that one. I'll do the corners. I'm great at the corners!" I asserted. After several breaks and accumulated paint splatters in our collective curls, I finished the last large walls with the roller by myself. The kids came out briefly and noted the immense change. I threw our mustard cover—dyed with coffee and turmeric—over our long-loved couch, now without an attached ottoman to fit the smaller room, and sent photos to my friends and family. "You're always so good at making a house feel like a home!" my friend Claude praised. The responses continued to pour in. Maybe the most powerful of them all, this one, also from Claude: "Your homes have a scent. Your clothes. Upstate too. And they all have the same *feeling*." That feeling, Claude would later express that July on my birthday, was the same one she got from being my friend. The same feeling of me. I had worked so hard on these places, places Claude had seen me birth alongside myself, even back to the summer of 2022 in that Berlin baptism— and in the house she came to paint with me, and in the apartment she helped me pass keys off to that same January.

"You're glowing," another friend said. Over and over again that day, I admitted: "I finally feel at home in myself." Home, notwithstanding a year of compassion. I said words that were Thomas Merton's to myself and to others like a prayer that entire year, switching from the previous year's meditation. I repeated them in the days leading up to the Mae House gathering, just as I did during those spring break mornings with the kids, and while navigating relationships with lovers and exes, with friends I no longer kept, with my mother, and with my father, too—whose life and loss resurfaced for me that same year of the Mae House's first anniversary. This relationship also found its way back to its own home.

Then it was as if I suddenly saw the secret beauty of their hearts, the depths of their hearts where neither sin nor desire nor self-knowledge can reach, the core of their reality, the person that each one is in God's eyes. If only they could see themselves as they really are. If only we could see each other that way all the time, there would be no more war, no more hatred, no more cruelty, no more greed . . . I suppose the big problem would be that we would fall down and worship each other.

—*Thomas Merton*

In my quest for home during the three years of this book's companionship, I spent many days rediscovering one simple truth: I couldn't run. What came from that was a true need and sense that I had to dive back in, greet others with compassion (both the living and gone), and most importantly, offer myself that same compassion. My restoration after that grief took an entire year. All things considered, this is short, I know. Hard work takes time, after all. The work, as I described of the house, too, is never quite done. But by that June of 2023, my work with my father—and ultimately with myself, in that regard—felt as if it had come to a close. I was in my home of homes.

Serendipity is a noun, described as the effect by which one accidentally stumbles across something truly wonderful, especially while looking for something truly unrelated. That February, before that April and before that June, my mother had continued her prayers for me. Not only that I would settle into my home but that I'd find work that would offer me peace and ultimately ease. And that May, a friend whom I had been estranged from for two years (including one that preceded the purchase of the house) walked back into my life. Not because they hadn't always been there but because grief is a funny thing. It allows you—however painful—to assess your own misgivings. And that friend, as my friend likes to say, closed a karmic circle with a job—a job that not only was part of the restoration of our friendship but also of me.

As June arrived and my first work trip to Dakar and Ghana was nearing, I ordered a DNA test—which I had desired to do for some time. The test results arrived a week before I was set to take off, and I opened them in the booth of a French café I often spend my mornings at catching up on emails. I was 80 percent West African, only two to four generations away from Ghanaian. The other 20 percent was a running record of my mother's history as a woman whose own lineage was evidence of the sanctuary of New York. I bent over in shock, crying, heaving, breathing mostly not at all while on the phone with my friend Rubi. "Breathe," she coaxed. "This is a lot." A stranger came to check on me. It was not as if someone died, but the feeling that crawled into my stomach, the relief that hit my chest, and the well that escaped my eyes felt as if my years of unanswered questions from my father were there via his overwhelming presence in that DNA test. I had always wondered about him—how he may have felt arriving here from Panama, whether he was also lost in that generation of migration. And, too, what he felt those last days leading to his death. Why he kept it quiet, and if he thought about us, me, in those final days and hours. In some strange way, the test offered answers I could no longer escape. It wasn't that I felt—ever truly—attached to this feeling of going "home" to West Africa, a complexity that Saidiya Hartman explores in her work. However, it was that I just wasn't aware of how and why it was uniquely important for me until I arrived. Those answers and that importance could only be found *if* I were ever able to follow the long path to make it.

"Welcome home," the man at the airport said as I trailed behind our fixer. "He

says that to everyone, I bet," the photographer accompanying me on this work trip whispered back, unfazed by it and my amazement. It wasn't the statement, it was that I saw my father so clearly in nearly every man I saw. *There.* And *there.* During a swift seventy-two hours, I allowed my mind to quiet at the foot of the Atlantic. I was overtaken by an undeniable motion to move with whatever was presented to me. The next thing was always the right thing. I watched the sun rise and set, and grasped tightly to what I could only describe as an offering from my father, one that he couldn't give me in his own aliveness and in his death. Or maybe you'll read this and see it as serendipity. Characterized by my hopes and my dreams. Ghana, however brief, posited answers and offered an openness within myself that wasn't there prior to my trip.

I got back to New York and spent two days dancing with friends in my new Brooklyn backyard as other friends headed to the Mae House for weeks of rejuvenation and healing of their own. The kids and I flew to Paris, then to Berlin, where I wrote about the West Africa trip and the creatives I met for my work assignment while my children played in the next room. We spent our days exploring museums. And on my birthday, I swam again in the Schlachtensee with my children and a few friends—including one who flew in from Brooklyn with my favorite doughnut as my birthday cake. "How does it feel to be out of your Jesus year?" my mother asked me.

"Wonderful! I love you, Mommy," I responded.

The next day, my friend Katherine and I went to get tattoos. She knew someone who may be available. Serendipitous, I told her. On a piece of paper, River wrote the word *BE.* Then I wrote, *HERE.* Finally, Oak wrote, *NOW.* River, the water that began this journey. Here, the anchor—me—that will steady us. And with Oak, the realization that I always need to stay rooted. The tattoo artist took our handwritten words and transferred them onto tracing paper, and I placed it on the inside of my forearm. The same forearm that lies below my children as they've slept and cuddled for nearly thirteen years. The forearm I often see when I pause from writing. It is a forever reminder to be in this body, with these children, with this work.

Just as I have been here, with you, now.

Acknowledgments

In a 2017 conversation with Thich Nhat Hanh, bell hooks writes: "Love is always the place where I begin and end." And as will I.

Over the course of the last four years, it was a belief and love of bell hooks's world and work that has guided my own work and my heart. She passed away during a season in which I needed her work the most. A season in which I am sure many of us needed her. And in her passing, and in my grief, it was hooks, the thought of my children, and my meditation that kept me quite literally alive during a few dark weeks. Weeks during which this book needed to be paused, and the finishing of it felt impossible. I think here always of my grandmother: "Joy comes in the morning." For River and Oak, for being my evenings, but mostly my mornings. A reminder of a life worth living and a life lived well. A life of adventure, of art, of forgiveness, and of deep love. Of being taught and of being the teacher at every minute of the day.

In that same piece, Hanh shares, "Community is the core of everything." To be in community with you, the readers, has been a gift, made possible only by my immediate community: Tony, Damāār, Brittany, Dario, my nieces and nephews (there are too many to name), Uncle, Auntie, Aunt Maine, great-aunts—my great-aunt Peggy, especially. And in my dreams, my clothes, Brooklyn, and the air we chart, Bertha Mae Vaughn, and "Mommy" Margaret Baker, who brought her into this world to be shared with many of us. Now you are in this work, too.

"I am with you just as you have been with me, and we encourage each other to realize our deepest love, caring and generosity . . . together on the path of love," Sister Chan Khong writes in her book *Learning True Love*. Together and chosen, Joylynn Holder, Sarah Ann Noel, Sarah Sophie Flicker and Jesse Peretz, Christy DeGallerie, Casey Miller, Rubi Aguilar, Autumn Standford, Rita Nakouzi, Jenna Gribbon, Alexa Wilding, Whitney Ortiz, Kahlila, Dr. L, Danielle Coon, Cherokee Lynn, Nicole Gonzalez, Claude Viard, Erin Boyle, Lauren Lamborne, Phenia Jean Pierre, Lynn Slater, Christine Platt, April Gariepy, and Nina Elsbeth along with many others.

Breath is the key to a mindful practice. And so, this book is broken into two sections: an inhale and exhale. An opportunity to look in and out. To notice (and not be distracted by) what we may not control. Much of that has been achieved only by the hands of my working community of which I'll name: Lauren Shonkoff, Max Stein, Andrianna deLone, Maya Millett, Bee and Rog Walker, and finally, Chayenne Skeete for first imagining this book alongside me.

bell hooks was a devout Christian-Buddhist, and in such a way, I have felt at ease in my own journey of mixing past childhood teachings and an overall spiritual practice. To Katherine, Skye, Michelle, Sharleene, and everyone I met as I made my way: thank you for holding my hand by the water; the memory to always swim back to myself in baptism and in beauty.

For Daddy, a man I no longer search for in his death, but finally know in this life of forgiveness. Thank you.

Finally, for my mother, Tonya. To carry a portion of your name, your art, and all of what you gave in my heart and thoughts each day is a gift I am so grateful to fully realize. I thank you for being my first home and lesson on how to always find my way back.

LATONYA YVETTE is a multimedia storyteller who writes the news-letter "With Love, L." Yvette's first book, *Woman of Color,* was included in an installation of Jay-Z's personal bookshelf for Brooklyn Public Library's *Book of HOV* exhibit. She also co-authored the illustrated children's book *The Hair Book* with Amanda Jane Jones. Yvette is the owner and steward of the Mae House, an upstate New York rental property and the home of Rest as Residency, which offers BIPOC families a no-cost place for rest and focus.

latonyayvette.com
latonyayvette.substack.com
Instagram: @latonyayvette

Books Driven by the Heart

Sign up for our newsletter and find more you'll love:

thedialpress.com

@THEDIALPRESS

@THEDIALPRESS